D1552805

IT'S BEST IF YOU DON'T REACH OUT

The unexceptional late thirties male against COVID-19, genital
herpes, and $18 an hour employment

by Jason Kinkade
Author of "Social Sex" (2014)

jason.deinosuchus@gmail.com

jason.hesperornis@gmail.com

jason.parasaurolophus@gmail.com

jason.sarcosuchus@gmail.com

Table of Contents

INTRODUCTION

INTRODUCTION

Part 1

I'm a poop criminal

First of all, I'm a poop criminal.

I was on a date at one of Tucson's three malls, and sometime between dinner at that generic chain restaurant and bowling at that arcade that plays royalty free music I felt a familiar, but feared judder in my stomach. My irritable bowel syndrome is usually more active in the morning, and then diminishes during the day, but this night I made the poor choice to continue drinking beer. The speed of service was severely impacted by a lack of people willing to work in the restaurant industry following everything we learned about labor, wages, and the wealthy over the course of the pandemic. So to avoid looking awkward I kept drinking beer while our food languished in the understaffed kitchen, and triggered my IBS just before we got on a lane.

"I'm going to go buy us some beers," I said to my date as she laced up her bowling shoes. She looked confused because we just drank so many beers next door, and logically I should be gearing up to bowl, too. Instead, I left my shoes in a heap and took off toward the concessions. When I confirmed I was no longer in her line of sight, I veered off toward the stairwell. I needed to run downstairs to the restrooms, evacuate my bowels, clean myself with a wet paper towel (habit, but also necessary when you wipe excessively all day like I do), run back upstairs, and buy two beers before resuming our date. Some events needed to break my way for this to not appear unusual, including an available stall in the men's room followed by a short line to purchase alcohol.

Do Not Enter. Closed For Cleaning.

"Fuck!" I whispered to myself, as I approached the sporting arena style restrooms. There was one large subway looking entrance for men, and another large subway looking entrance for women (no doors, just hallways). The men's entrance had a shower rod extended across the middle with every frequent flyer's nightmare notification hanging from it: This restroom is unavailable. I yelled, "Hello...?" hoping a sympathetic employee might grant me passage, but none answered. I watched a couple and then a few women exit the other restroom, and started considering how many women might still be in there and what would be the consequence for claiming gender fluidity.

"Screw this!" I psyched myself up, and darted under the little beam that stood between me and the solution to shitting myself on my date. As soon as I rounded the corner, I startled the referee costumed employee standing in the middle of the room who then began waving his arms side-to-side like he was going to eject me from a baseball game. "Hey man," I started to explain as I dodged past him and his outstretched arms, "I drank a lot of beer, my stomach is upset, and I'm having an emergency!" I closed the stall door, and sat on the toilet. I immediately expelled a torrent of gas, and felt instant relief. No shit this time, just another annoying false alarm. As my mind calculated how much time I wasted pretending to buy beer, I heard the referee call security.

I listened incredulously to this little bastard tell his radio, "I need security in the men's room because a guy just breached the barricade!" Are you kidding me? Breached the barricade? "And now he's sitting in the stall that's clogged." OK that's bad, but he could have pointed me to a safe throne! I frantically wiped away the clear goo that leaves the asshole in false alarms, and shouted back, "I didn't do anything, it was just gas!" I left my stall, and started washing my hands, but the uncompromising staff continued his distress call, "Yeah, now he's washing his hands. He's like five' eight with dark hair..." I figured the likeliest outcome now was my date ending in embarrassment, and weighed the morality of just going home, unmatching this woman from the app, and never returning to the mall.

As I breached the barricade out of the bathroom, and reemerged in the downstairs arcade, I immediately locked eyes with two mall security guards making their way to me. They were still a ways away, so I ran between the colorful and noisy video games, and started zig-zagging my way back to the stairwell. "This is humiliating," I thought to myself, wondering why the jerk in the bathroom couldn't relate to another human in need or at least appreciate me not taking a dump he would have to clean up in front of his precious barricade. I decided to go back to my date, and told her the line to buy beers was too long. She looked over my shoulder, and said, "Um… I can go try in a minute," as clearly only a smattering of people were buying food. I noticed she had entered our names on the scoreboard.

So we bowled. And while we bowled, the two security guards stood about ten feet back and watched us for probably six turns. My date never knew I was a poop criminal, but I live with the shame.

Part 2

What even is this book?

Simply put, this book is the therapy journal of an unexceptional late thirties male who was impacted by COVID-19, even though he never caught COVID (yet), impacted by genital herpes, even though he isn't infected by genital herpes (yet), and impacted by $18 an hour employment, even though he doesn't want to work $18 an hour employment. Like, ever. Ew.

As this is a therapy journal, you should recognize the effort as such. I'll try to keep typos to a minimum, but some are going to make it to publication. I also have a problem with malapropisms, so, yeah, just have fun with those when you find them. What's a malapropism? A malapropism is a word mistaken for a similar looking or sounding word (so spell check won't help). Effect, affect. Allude, elude. Compliment, complement. Angel, angle. This warning is here because of the criticism the first love of my life heaped upon my other book (hey, you), but we're friends now so it's cool. In her defense, the other book wasn't kind to her. And in one of my futile attempts to win her back, she threw in my face, "Jason, you wrote an entire book about why you don't want to be with me." The other book was also a therapy journal.

Every so many years I get depressed enough to either kill myself or start therapy journaling. Regrettably, the first time I felt compelled to move my ruminating thoughts from my tortured mind to the page, I published the book under my real name. I was just out of college, but working at a big box retailer because low and behold college doesn't really guarantee the opportunities we were promised growing up. My degrees are in journalism and history, and since my class projects had me reporting from the southern border, I was naturally able to start a career in social work. While social work doesn't pay a living wage, at least for awhile I felt more fulfilled than I did stocking shelves. Unfortunately, that book loomed over me as a search result if anybody queried my name. I had written cringey stories about being lonely, difficulties fitting in through high school and college, and tried to thread my coming-of-age journey through the theme of growing up in the first generation with home Internet access. Sounds fine, but I whined like an incel, and, when talking about exploring the early chat rooms, even defined my goal as searching for "slutty bitches."

Are you kidding me, past-self? Why would you write that? And, having written that, why would you leave your name on top? For the record, I am the only slutty bitch I know. I am promiscuous, and, while I try to be kind, my depression and anxiety sometimes impair me from fully showing up for the people counting on me. I hold women in high regard, and am firmly on the side of /r/FemaleDatingStrategy. I matured slower than what is ideal, and carried my teenage boy mentality into those early adult years.

So that was book one.

Book two also doesn't stand up to scrutiny, but at least I had the good sense to use the pseudonym I am using for this book. After receiving zero attention from the opposite sex in high school and college, I was suddenly bombarded with flirtations while working in a female dominated field (social work, if you forgot). And, detrimental to my mental health, I eagerly engaged with the attention. The catalyst for this round of therapy journaling was the first love of my life telling me she got off the merry-go-round and was dating somebody else. Until then, I thought we would be on again and off again until we righted our relationship for good. That was my first crushing heartbreak, and my choice was either kill myself or write about it. Luckily that book didn't loom over me as a search result if anybody queried my name. I had written cringey stories about getting hella laid, difficulties fitting into relationships, and tried to thread my sexual experiences through the theme of online dating before we had the apps (back when you still needed a computer and a completely filled out profile). Sounds fine, but I had an older male coworker, just two of us in an office of 20 women, egging me into taking more dates just so I'd have fresh stories. I think I wrote my miniseries extra salaciously just for him. When I pick up the book today, I am mostly ashamed of myself, but, also grateful that I have a record of memories I might otherwise forget.

So that was book two.

Book three honestly isn't so bad, and is the only time killing myself wasn't in the equation. I was a supervisor for a semi-independent placement for older boys in foster care, and we had a habit of always putting together discharge binders with the same resources. Eventually I asked the other supervisors of similar programs to send me all the tips and contacts they were providing in their efforts to transition young adults from congregate care to functional adulthood, and I compiled everything in a total life skills book. I sorted out topics, provided the links, addresses, and phone numbers, and then wrote summaries for each step in transitioning to adulthood. For example, "Employment" was made up of chapters on job searching, resumes, networking, interviewing, boasting about soft skills if work history is lacking (remember my audience is teens), maintaining employment, building motivation, and how to quit a job. I even covered those annoying aptitude tests a lot of the online applications require where you have to choose between nonsense like, "Which sounds more like you: Do you believe in giving the greatest customer service of your life or do you believe in living as the human expression of the brand you represent?" This book was a real banger, but none of the youth in my program wanted to read it.

So that was book three.

Here we are at book four. Why am I therapy journaling again? To stave off those pesky suicidal ideations one more time. I am heartbroken beyond belief, but this time I did everything right and still lost. This time I wasn't an entitled incel like I was in book one, I wasn't a womanizer like I was in book two, I wasn't without the life skills for success thanks to book three, but I still hit rock bottom. I am going to write cringey stories about being lonely, difficulties incumbent to the unexceptional late thirties male experience, and try to thread my first year teaching high school through the greater theme of the COVID pandemic. And I also want to preserve a little bit of love that was lost.

Getting the words completely right isn't the point of this book.

Part 3

The years 2019, 2020, 2021

My timeline isn't exact, but I needed to organize my experiences in an order I could write about. When I say it's 2019, 2020, and 2021 I am referring to the main event that defined that year for me. The stories themselves bleed into the years on either side. Obviously, COVID-19 came in waves, and everybody knows a school year doesn't line up perfectly with a calendar year. Like with the typos and malapropisms please just roll with my exposition.

The rising action in my 2019 was losing both my home and my job, and getting assaulted by a former coworker. This is a trigger warning for sexual assault. That part is not a joke. While this whole attempt at book writing might be a joke, my sexual assault is not. I was touch averse for a long time after it happened, and think I still suffer from some PTSD. The climax that defined my 2019 was getting everything I lost back and better than before. The cascade of events that pulled me out of homelessness, an abusive situation, and into a job I truly enjoyed showing up for amounted to pure luck. Unfortunately, the resolution to my 2019 was that COVID took it all away again.

The rising action in my 2020 was becoming a fake teacher. I started out wanting to be a real teacher, but the education machine in Arizona is just too broken to be fixed from the inside. I also started dating with pandemic precautions, but was held back by wanting to relive some specific childhood and adolescent trauma. The climax that defined my 2020 was accepting that my charter school hired me to commit fraud, and leaning into the scam completely. The charter school for which I worked did not care if we taught anything as long as we wrote credit slips. We worked for a business, not an educational institution, that provided a very specific service. We were a printing press for unearned high school diplomas intended for students who would otherwise fall through the cracks, fulfilling the government's objective that there are never adults unable to apply for menial labor and minimum wage jobs. Unfortunately, the resolution to my 2020 was falling in love with a woman who waited a ridiculously long time to tell me something important. By the time she finally confessed, I was already emotionally invested and could not choose to not be in love.

The rising action in my 2021 was becoming a real counselor and teacher. Obviously, if I could undo the deaths of everybody who died from COVID I would happily give up any of the gains I acquired in the pandemic response. That weird fake teaching detour the pandemic put me on finally swerved back to my regular path, and all the economic stimulus payments put my bank account firmly in the black. I finally had the comfortable unhappiness back that was more familiar to me as a social worker than the anxious and almost unbearable unhappiness I had trying to make sense of teaching in a charter school. The climax that defined my 2021 was crippling depression. I've only been in love twice. My first girlfriend was with me, if I use fuzzy math, for eight months. My second girlfriend was with me, if I use even fuzzier math (and she might dispute the title girlfriend since we only ever used the word exclusive), for three months. If you add up my two experiences being in a loving relationship I almost have a whole year as a real man. Even though we broke up before I resumed my regular employment, the crushing sadness from losing the second love of my life didn't hit until three months later. Unfortunately, the resolution to my 2021 was writing another terrible book to avoid killing myself.

Part 4

A brief history of adolescent trauma

I need to share two really embarrassing facts about me that come up in Part 19 and Part 33. I was bullied relentlessly at every grade of school from K through 12. I remember early on crying to my parents that I did not want to go back to the classroom because the other kids never stopped making fun of me. My well meaning dad said I just needed to bring donuts the next day, and doing so would make me popular and everybody's new friend. I vaguely remember my peers eating my donuts and kicking the shit out of me. I guess I don't blame them because I was pretty awkward. I walked with a weird gait, I wanted my hair to be longer and cool, but it was longer and weird, I wanted my glasses to look like my dad's pair, but that style frame looked weird on a little kid, and everything I said came out awkward and weird. A teacher was assigning groups, in a grade that followed my peace offering of donuts, and after she publicly added my name to a forming team, one of the kids already grouped, yelled, "No! He's so gay, I swear!" And what struck me as odd was that this particular kid seemed nice and had never bullied me before. And the girls? Just as bad if not worse. Girls would dare each other to hug me or tell me they liked me, and then follow that with rip-roaring hilarious laughter. When you spend your whole life hearing you're a piece of shit unworthy of love you start to believe it, and while I don't hold any ill will or even remember the names of most the bullies I do believe their harassment is part of my main problem today. I've resented people for showing me affection, thinking if someone likes a piece of shit like me there must be something wrong with them.

In Part 19 of this book, I tell women offering me no strings attached sex that I am a virgin just to see how they react. When I was in high school, all the little idiots suddenly became obsessed with who was or wasn't having sex. There were probably only a few males getting laid, but most of the other males were probably savvy enough to fake it until they made it. So that left me, who only wanted to be left alone, to absorb all the ridicule. Even when I escaped to a private school (smaller classrooms, religious themes) in hopes of not being bullied, I was still the butt of every joke told about virginity. I was absolutely horrified at the time, but as an adult I've been stuck somewhat turned on thinking about how invested women were in not having sex with me. So as pathetic as it sounds, I've told a couple women that I'm a later in life virgin just to see what they do with the information. Some of the responses are actually pretty hot.

In Part 33 of this book, I wear basic white underwear before a sexual encounter just to see if the woman will laugh or go through with the lovemaking. When I was in middle school, all the little idiots suddenly became obsessed with who was or wasn't wearing colorful boxer shorts. I'm not sure if the boys had a meeting over the summer, but I never got the memo. Furthermore, when I told my mom I needed a different style underwear she told me the pairs I already owned in excess were sufficient. So be it. For the longest time, I had to hurriedly get dressed before and after gym while wearing perfectly comfortable underwear that had inexplicably fallen out of fashion. I figure the boys who saw me changing sold me out to the girls, who then sought me out to confirm and then mock my basic white underwear. I was absolutely horrified at the time, but as an adult I've been stuck somewhat turned on thinking about just how invested women were in my embarrassing underwear. I've wanted to put on a pair before having sex for the first time with a new partner, but never gone through with it (until now) because I wasn't willing to risk increased performance anxiety or a missed sexual opportunity just to see what would happen. The response when I finally did was actually pretty hot.

Still I would rather not have this trauma inside me.

Part 5

Life goals

This is my last year as an unexceptional late thirties male. Next year I'll be an unexceptional early forties male. All I really want to do now is:

Resolve my childhood, adolescent, and adult trauma and access a rewarding relationship. People do like me, I'm always popular at work, but I have few friends and am suspicious of potential partners who try to get to know me. I think the best thing I do as a social worker and counselor is help teens gain confidence in themselves. As a victim of intense bullying, I know how eager trauma is to follow you through every next stage of your life. The funny thing about my bullies from high school, though, is that all their youthful good looks melted away while my slightly below average looks held up incredibly well. This is the case every time I run into somebody I used to know. Unfortunately, I'm still reeling from the intense heartbreak of losing the second love of my life. I needed four years to get over the eight month relationship I shared with the first love of my life. Now I'm trying to will myself, in a fraction of the time, over the three month relationship I shared with the second love of my life.

I want to blow the whistle on that Arizona charter school. Seriously email me if you're a reporter, and I'll tell you which school I worked at that still commits an egregious amount of fraud. I uploaded evidence to myself when I left in case I was scapegoated in an audit after getting a new job. I can show you all the instances where students passed credit recovery pre-tests in a matter of minutes not hours, and finished credit classes in hours not weeks. Don't get me wrong, I do think students who otherwise wouldn't graduate should have an easy pass option, but the experience I will write about reveals a corporate office insulating itself from blame while applying pressure on teachers to put themselves and their certifications at risk. I also recorded the principal saying dumb racist shit.

I want to reform the government so we can all climb out of the grinder. All this time I thought I was going to work because, like every other animal on earth, the choice was wake up and fight like hell or starve to death. Thanks to COVID-19, we now know that the economy creates enough wealth to meet everyone's basic needs, and nobody should be working a 40 hour work week. And nobody should be working a 40 hour work week and not taking home enough pay to meet their needs. We should all be receiving a universal basic income, and then venturing out to earn more if we want to earn more. We should live most of our life exploring nature, creating art, and enjoying relationships. Apparently the system could have been turned off at any time, but stayed on so a few assholes could own extra jets and yachts. Now even though I like my job, I'm solidly in the "fuck you, pay me" mindset. And even though I'm proud of my social work, what families need more than me are direct cash payments. Tax the billionaires for the sake of our planet and our sanity.

Is that too much to ask?

2019

I LOSE MY JOB AND MY HOME

Part 6

I rage quit my job, and have nowhere to work

For four years, I supervised a semi-independent group home for older teen boys about to leave foster care. They were no longer "cute enough" to get adopted, and we needed to imbue them with life skills, a high school diploma, a job and a chance. The statistic remains 50 percent of all foster youth will end up homeless. Only two percent will graduate from college. I never wanted to work in a group home again after my first experience, not that it was bad, just that it was depressing and time consuming (no holidays, for example, because you can't pause somebody's life to celebrate a federal day off). But then I was more or less recruited to run a "semi-independent" group home. The difference was that the five boys living in my group home would have had to succeed at the lower tiers of homes (like the feeder property that housed up to 20 boys). Most the time I could even interview the boys first, so they knew they were committing to going to school, using public transportation, working a part time job, shopping for themselves on a weekly stipend, doing chores, and contributing to the greater good. I told them if they were going to do illegal shit just do it off site and not involve me or the house. I had a ton of time to myself when all five residents were working and going to school. For most of those years, life was good for all of us.

All of us meaning the five boys, myself, and my two staff. I typically worked 10 a.m. to 6 p.m. Monday through Friday, with an overnight staff who worked 6 p.m. to 10 a.m. Monday through Thursday (he slept there), and a weekend staff who worked from Friday at 6 p.m. until Monday at 10 a.m. (he also slept there). My two staff could actually end a shift whenever they got the last boy out the door for school, though. They would text me that the house was empty, and I wouldn't have to come in until around the time school ended. My weekend staff was an interesting hire. The other houses in our programs had the two non-management staff sharing the weeknights and then each taking one weekend day, but my house had this unique schedule of a full time weekend staff because he was an older man who liked being off all week. He wasn't seasoned in the foster care business, and it was better he didn't talk to anybody's guardian from the Department of Child Safety during the week. He was every boy's favorite staff because he said yes to everything, and gave tons of rides so they wouldn't have to use the bus. Part of my speech to new residents was, "If you like having somebody chill all weekend then don't take advantage of him." And nobody who lived with us long term ever did. A couple short termers took the group home car for joy rides on weekend guy's watch.

Of all the boys who lived at our group home over the years, there is a small group that stays in touch with me. One young man was exceptionally gifted. Like prodigy level gifted. When you're in charge of a youth edification program, and suddenly you have somebody with genius level talent and intellect you feel a certain pressure to develop them. I made sure our group home had resident computers, a piano, and other amenities this young man needed to grow his abilities. I even took him to dance lessons one night a week during my off time. He also left the group home with over $50,000 in pledged scholarship money (this is in addition to his foster care tuition waiver), and moved directly into the dorms at the University of Arizona. All that money came from him carefully applying to everything for which he was entitled, such as essay contests big and small, and anything to do with being a minority or LGBTQ member. You will see him in the preforming arts some day. He was also a diva, and annoyed the hell out of me, but we respected each other and made it work. Weekend guy provided him driving lessons in the group home car, which was definitely illegal, and they both lied to me that the smashed taillight "just happened" while they were at the grocery store. So for the right youth, moving into our group home was an incredible opportunity. We three adults were supportive, and flexible with rules, and the five boys were appreciative, and either followed rules or kept their illegal shit off site. Some of the other boys, now grown, have moved all over the country and are doing well.

The collapse of our way of life came when the system stopped producing qualifying youth. Towards the end of my reign, there were no more boys at the feeder property that I wanted to move in after interviewing them. They were mostly maladaptive, manipulative and violent. Still, we as an agency couldn't survive with empty beds, so boys started being moved in based on openings and not merit. Whereas before I could carefully select candidates from the feeder property, now they were flung at me straight from jail. I'm not even talking about juvenile detention. One boy beat up his mom with a video game console power cable, went to jail for domestic violence, then moved into my group home. I remember protesting to my boss, "I thought we were a semi-independent placement for youth wanting an opportunity to join society, not a flop house for men who beat women." And about this video game console he brought with him, as soon as he connected it to our wireless Internet the thing alerted its real owner and we were raided by cops. Not shortly after this guy showed up, we had his best friend move in with us, too. Then the police came and took molds of the bottom of their shoes because some houses got robbed in the neighborhood, and victims were reporting stolen firearms.

Fuck that, I quit. Shortly after I quit my semi-independent group home, the whole concept was dissolved. The agency picked up the government's more lucrative unaccompanied minor contracts, and housed some of those youth Trump separated from their families at the border. The official protocol when an unaccompanied minor turned 18 was to call ICE. The unofficial protocol when an unaccompanied minor turned 18 was to blow out birthday candles and then give them a head start before calling ICE. I was happy to be gone, but unfortunately I left without a new job prospect.

Part 7

I rage quit my apartment, and have nowhere to live

My first solo living space since moving away from my parents at the tender age of late-twenties-something was a clean and fresh one bedroom apartment in the Foothills. The complex was one of those sprawling mirages where the leasing people drive you in a golf cart to a delicately decorated model to give you a false impression of luxury. Still, I had a nice view of the Santa Catalina mountain range, a fitness center, two swimming pools, two laundry mats, and all the shopping and restaurants I liked within walking distance. Most the sex stories in my second book took place at this apartment. The maintenance man was a player like me (haha). He would roll up in his golf cart as he saw me coming and going just to boast about his latest conquest. He was older than me, had long hair, and hid his beer belly under rock band shirts. I did see him making out with babes late at night so I knew his stories were legit. Whether I was with or without company, I had a favorite Baja Mexican restaurant at the corner I could walk to, order delicious chicken nachos, drink two Rum Runners, and stumble home. Note- In today's time, I just revisited this place, and a single Rum Runner knocked me on my ass. Don't ever get old, people. Anyway, I lived at these apartments for seven or eight great years.

My apartment was downstairs and for five of those years I never heard any of my revolving upstairs neighbors. Once I had a goofy paranoid proto-Karen up there who would descend to knock on my door and ask if I was smoking marijuana because the imaginary odor was wafting and seeping into her unit. Nope, it's all in your head. I didn't mind assuaging her concerns, and her visits didn't bother me in the least (again, we didn't know what a Karen was yet). Another time I had a bunch of teens up there, probably sharing rent between the handful of them, who would come downstairs and ask if it were OK if they threw a party. No problem, have fun! And I still didn't hear them or any evidence of the party. I think they probably just played fantasy card games since a couple of them always wore anime ears and tails. Another time yet, I had a single middle age guy who would occasionally ask for help hauling a sofa he found in the dumpster upstairs, and I'd happily oblige. He wasn't weird for doing this because more often than not we all pulled our furniture from the dumpster. Whenever I got tired of a piece of furniture in my apartment I'd just drag it out there and then wait for something new and interesting to appear. The circle of life. Again, five of these years were great.

And then the hillbillies from hell moved in above me. These dirty old hermits backed in two huge green vans that blocked my view of the Santa Catalinas, and then never moved them. When I noticed a flat tire that hadn't been changed for months, I tried to report that particular van to the county as abandoned. I was later notified that the license and registration were current. I was immediately aware that I lived downstairs because the sudden and unrelenting stomping never ever stopped. Stomp. Stomp. Stomp. All night long. And because the hillbillies never left the apartment, I never had a break. They also cooked constantly, and so in addition to stomping I heard them beating up the kitchen. Clang. Bang. Bump. All day long. The most irritating noise by far was their ensemble of backwoods instruments. I heard around-the-clock strumming of guitars, beating of drums, and whistling of… empty jugs? Pluck. Pow. Peeew! I steadily turned into a crazy person.

First, I walked upstairs, knocked on the door, and asked if they would not play instruments when I was home. They offered that when they got too loud I could come back and let them know. I said they're always too loud if I am home, and they said they would figure out some soundproofing for me. They never did. Then I sent letters, but took care to make the writing look like multiple neighbors were complaining. Unfortunately, the longer the hillbillies lived above me the more friends they made. They were popular with anyone who didn't share a wall or floor because they gave away so much of that gross slop they cooked. They would camp out on their balcony and announce to any passerby that they had stew or squash or some shit to give away. Gross slop. The old man never wore a shirt, so I was treated to a view of his weird little nips poking off his frail body. He also had a long and wispy white beard exactly how hillbillies are drawn when they are a punchline in a cartoon. I got so nauseated that I bought a pack of t-shirts and tossed it up there. The old lady, clothed in overalls and wearing gray pigtails, would sometimes try to win me over by shouting niceties from the balcony, but I just wanted to be able to come and go in peace. I threw lots of objects at my ceiling, but they never shut the fuck up.

Obviously I complained to management. I complained, and complained, and complained. Eventually the leasing office stopped taking my calls, so I left messages, after messages, after messages. But the thing about these enormous manufactured apartment complexes where they take you to the perfect model on a golf cart is that they don't give a fuck about you once you're paying rent. I was eloquently told to fuck off a million ways before being ignored entirely. My favorite line of bullshit was always being offered a more expensive unit somewhere upstairs. Um, no, move me up there for the same price I pay now since I'm being assaulted with hillbilly noise every waking moment. Although in hindsight, rent back then was completely reasonable compared to what we pay in the post-COVID-19 society. And obviously, in addition to complaining to management, I called 911. A lot. I called 911 a whole lot. I'd always request not to have contact with the deputy, and go back to bed. But I'd hear the sheriff walk upstairs, chat with the hillbillies a little, then leave. Nothing ever changed other than the leasing office and sheriff's department were both logging how much I complained and building a case that I was the nuisance. Once the hillbillies' drug addled adult son moved in, they were empowered to fight back and started complaining about me complaining about them. Now if I threw objects at the ceiling, the drug addled adult son would slam down something heavy to retaliate.

I was already gearing up for a fight with the office about a month before I needed to renew my lease, but then when the letter finally appeared on my door it said I no longer qualified for another year. In all the years past, that letter said if I wanted to renew I would need to agree to a $20 increase, I'd then go and argue, and the office would eventually renege and let me sign up for another year at the same rate. For five years I was a perfect tenant, and then for two years I couldn't be because I never got a moment of peace away from the horrible hillbillies. Even though I just bought a $1,000 queen bed, I hatched a plan to disappear in the middle of the night. I was not going to give my gross backwoods tormentors the satisfaction of sitting on their balcony smoking marijuana while watching me lug and haul my belongings and furniture into a moving van. I started taking items I didn't want to throw away to the group home I still worked at for safekeeping (although since you read the previous part you know that my employment was simultaneously ending), and started packing clothes and necessities into four or five duffle bags as succinctly as possible. When I was able to fit the entirety of what was left of my life into my car, I waited for a lull in the upstairs music then fled through the dark of night. I was happy to be gone, but unfortunately I left without a new apartment prospect.

Part 8

I get a Jewish landlady and an obese housemate

To escape the apartments quickly, all I had to do was look at community sourced housing posts on a local message board. The first place I called was actually the place where I moved. I had never rented a room before, but the message just said for $400 a month I could have a room to myself, Wi-Fi, a shared bathroom, space in the fridge, and parking on the driveway. The neighborhood was near where my parents lived, and I figured moving in with such a light load of belongings would make it easier to ultimately get back on my feet quickly. The ad was posted by an extremely nice, but somewhat naive, Jewish lady. When I called, she told me the first person she meets face-to-face who also brings her cash gets the room. I raced over there, and reserved the room. She didn't check my background at all, didn't care that I offered up a fingerprint clearance card from my jobs in foster care, only wanted me to know she had a bizarre set of rules that governed coming and going, that she was frugal, and I was to never, ever, touch the A/C. My room was clean, already minimally furnished, and I slept very peacefully that first night. My new Jewish landlady was a retired surgeon's assistant, very involved in the community and her synagogue, and I kid you not belonged to a motorcycle gang that celebrated having conquered cancer. Yeah, she was cool as hell, and to this day she still calls me on my birthday. She also spent a lot of time in Israel, so I would have gotten this big house all to myself if it weren't for this new arrangement's one glaring inconvenience.

My Jewish landlady rented her other spare bedroom to this fat fuck named Stanley. Now, Stanley was a nice man, just morbidly obese. I didn't meet him immediately, because for one thing he worked nights at one of the greedier high speed Internet conglomerates, and for another thing he liked traveling to sporting games, and he took his hobby seriously. He would plan the trips well in advance and then rent cars so his own vehicle wouldn't rack up miles. Him renting a car always threw our three person parking plan out of whack, but at least it meant he would be gone for awhile. I was lying on my bed with the door open the first time Stanley lumbered home, and after we exchanged a formal greeting ("what's up, bro?"), he waddled into our shared bathroom and unleashed the fury of a billion frying demons. From my bed, I was leaning my back on the wall that was shared with the bathroom, and I swear it rolled and rolled in a manner by which buildings are constructed to withstand earthquake damage. The smells reached me before he even finished or opened the door. The bathroom was never habitable for hours after an assault by Stanley, and so I devised various ways to pee in my room and store liquids until disposing them was possible. The weirdest thing about Stanley visiting the bathroom was the unyielding archaeological deposits of toilet paper poop spirals. OK picture those common cone-shaped Gastropod fossils you always see next to Trilobites, and now imagine those made out of toilet paper and covered in feces. These fossils belonging to the record of his bowel movements always littered the floor after his mass extinction events. I guess when you're that obese wiping is a challenge, so I'm glad he tried, but the poop spirals were disgusting.

Somehow more than a year flew by, and I only started looking for a new place to live when I noticed myself wanting to get laid more. I suppose I needed all that time to recover from the hillbilly battles, and was just content jerking off in my cozy little bedroom. I did experience an accumulation of guilt for all the times I jizzed over carpet in a room I was only renting. I made a point to try and cum inside condoms, too, but I masturbated a lot (it's my main coping skill for stress, anger, and depression). Unfortunately, the first time I applied for a new apartment I discovered massive problems with my credit. Apparently the assholes at my old complex sent my remaining month to collections, as well as a bill for having to remove everything I abandoned. That made me mad, since they could have turned a profit selling the nicer stuff. Like I said before, the bed was new and cost me $1,000. I have never before or since owned a real bed, and I left it only lightly used. Enter a negative feedback loop where I would beg and plead my case to a random leasing office, get assured by sleazy landlords that they had my back, and then as soon as I paid another exorbitant application fee I would immediately be denied an apartment due to bad credit and a past lease break. Sometimes I'd still be walking to my car in the parking lot when the denial came. I started to think I might be sweeping up Stanley's poop spirals forever.

Part 9

I get assaulted by a former coworker

Life with the Jewish landlady and functionally handicapped fat man wasn't terrible, but I knew it could definitely be better. I knew by the lack of notifications on my phone that I had no friends to help me out. I was truly on my own until another batch of memes arrived from a former coworker who for some reason always curated crap from her social media and sent it to me in an unfunny stream. Now don't get me wrong, I enjoyed memes as much as anyone, but this former coworker's sense of humor seemed more attuned to what I assumed my hillbilly neighbors would think is funny (if they weren't illiterate hillbillies). You know those side panel advertisements on sketchy websites that depict famous cartoon characters having sex with each other? Those images tickled my former coworker's funny bone. While we weren't exactly friends, she was my most consistent texter. And if I was ever going to get out of my living arrangement with the Jewish landlady and functionally handicapped fat man then I was going to need a new landlady. I still couldn't rent anything on my own with shit credit and a lease break, but pay off those debts? Not a chance in hell. It's the principle (never bend to hillbillies or their enablers)!

My former coworker, Tammy, was about ten years older than me and very petite. She liked wearing tight clothes, and loudly looked down on bigger women. She could have been hot were it not for four decades of smoking taking its toll on her face, vocal cords, and lungs. Basically anything smoking could fuck up was fucked up on her. She was smart, but stupid, and with big resources. She was smart because she went to school long enough to get a particular Master's degree that pertained to our social work. She was dumb because she knew literally nothing else taught in school at any grade level. You could ask her who becomes president if the president and vice president die, and she wouldn't even understand the premise of the question. She had big resources because since the time she and I worked together she got a better job, and she bought a nice house in a cookie cutter development at the edge of the county. I didn't set out to take advantage of Tammy, but a consistent theme in her memes was about her being a single mom. So I started hitting her up in a way that was ambiguously flirtatious.

My strategy worked, and before too long Tammy was inviting me out for meals and movies, and then eventually dinners and beers, at her house. The first night I was at her house that coincided with a night her teenage daughter was with friends, I made my move and fucked the shit out of her. Tammy made gleeful comments the next day about how her pussy hurt so good. I found how she talked about her pussy all the time a turn off. I suppose I just saw too much hillbilly in her behavior, mannerisms, and comments to stay attracted for very long. The sex was OK, though (mostly doggy). After a few more encounters, I asked about the bedroom in the back. I pointed out that she was in the master bedroom, her daughter was in the second back bedroom, and that she had a third back bedroom without an occupant. Tammy told me that their dog was back there, and the room was empty except for the dog's crate, blanket, toys, food, and water. She said her daughter demanded a dog with the new house, but largely ignored the puppy because it was too hyper. She shared the plan was for the dog to get a little bigger and move outside. I told Tammy I paid my Jewish landlady $400 a month for a room, and that I'd pay her $500 a month for the dog's room if the dog could move outside sooner. Tammy almost immediately began cleaning weeks' worth of dog piss out of that third back bedroom.

Tammy stayed excited about me moving into the house, but got a little weird in those next couple weeks of preparation. I ordered furniture that got delivered straight to Tammy's house, and hurried over to build it. Tammy hovered the whole time, served plenty of beer (that was cool), but got pushy about sex. I told Tammy to leave me alone to focus, and reminded her that her daughter was home, but she yelled at the teen to take the dog for a walk. Then when the house was empty she tried to cajole me into following her to the master bedroom. I told her I wasn't comfortable banging her while knowing her daughter didn't have patience for the dog, and those walks frequently lasted all of five minutes. Tammy started picking up the cardboard boxes, along with all the flakes of debris from shipping and unpacking, and throwing everything away before I made any real progress assembling my desk and my nightstand. She wasn't a clean freak by any means just frustrated I wasn't focused on her. I introduced her to a new term for us that I hoped would catch on and provide me with some breathing room: "Roommates with benefits."

I just wanted to move into that third back bedroom, live a life parallel to Tammy's life, and occasionally come together for sex when we both wanted release. I had thought she was on the same page, but then she made a bizarre proposal on move-in day. "Are you all moved in?" She asked, checking on me as I connected my smart TV to her wireless Internet. Everything was a tight fit, but my room was mine, and I no longer shared a bathroom wall with the world's fattest man. I did already miss my Jewish landlady, though.

"I am moved in and very grateful, Tammy. Thank you!" I said, getting up to close the door so I could start my night.

"Great," Tammy continued, "Come sleep in my room."

"Uh, no, thank you, Tammy."

"Why?" She asked.

"Well, I just moved in tonight and I would like to get comfortable with my new room. I'm excited to have my own space, and I thank you again for this opportunity."

Tammy didn't go nuclear when I shut the door in her face, but she disappeared for awhile and said she would come back to say goodnight. When she did come back an hour later, she was wrapped in a towel and pushed her way inside my room. There she dropped the towel, and fucked me on my new roll-away bed. Her teenage daughter knocked, and demanded to know what we were up to together.

The daughter could not handle mom getting down. And while Tammy denied us doing so, the offspring wasn't as stupid as Tammy. Luckily, I no longer wanted to have sex with Tammy, so I figured the daughter taking a stand, and staying attached to Tammy's side, would end all that coerced lovemaking for good. Nope. Tammy just became more demanding of my time. Especially if my time coincided with the daughter not being home. I tried everything

I could think of to not be home, too, including bonding with the neglected dog and taking it on never ending walks (and the dog did in fact have boundless energy). Tammy reminded me upon my every return that she was providing me with a great deal, and, at this point, without her I would definitely be homeless. She was right, but now I was thinking in terms of nobody should have sex they don't want. When Tammy broke into my room again one night, drunk and coughing up cigarette smoke, I rolled over with a stern, "I do not consent."

"Shut the fuck up!" Tammy shouted, rolling me back over and climbing on top.

Goddamn it. I got raped.

Part 10

I discover substitute teaching is an instant-job

Many rapes later, Tammy confronted me with an absurd announcement. "Jason," She began like her comment wasn't going to be fucking stupid, "I thought over our relationship, and we need to start telling people we're partners."

"No."

"You've never liked the term boyfriend and girlfriend, but partners sounds more mature and carries a stronger meaning."

"I want to die."

Tammy also invented a new rule where I could pee and poop in the bathroom closest to my room, but due to that bathroom being where her daughter showered I had to take my showers in the master bedroom. That supposedly provided more privacy to the teen, but actually enabled Tammy to jump into my showers with me. She also installed a massaging shower head with a long cord for us.

I knew if I wanted to escape my captor I would need a job and some money. I heard on the radio that Arizona was desperate for substitute teachers, and that I could become one with little to no effort. When I called one of the districts, I found out this short path to teaching children was no joke (or the biggest joke). I literally had to take a handful of inconvenient, but ridiculously easy, steps and in about 20 minutes I could be a certified substitute in the state of Arizona for the entire next decade.

First, I went downtown during one of the two advertised days that the state's education office was even open. I waited in line with other questionable misfits, and showed that I possessed a Bachelor's degree in journalism and history (LMAO). Then I paid a small registration fee, and was given a certificate saying I was a substitute.

But wait, there's more. Second, I crossed the street to the recorder's office where a clerk stamped my certificate and handed it back to me with a raised seal and bag of treats. Bag of treats? Inside the bag of treats were some gimmicky stickers about teachers being valued, a mass produced thank you note from the governor, and a fun-sized candy bar (which I ate). My journey to become a substitute teacher had an unnecessary third step between the two I just described because when the instructions said bring a check I assumed that meant a voided check for my direct deposit. No, it was a blank check meant to pay the state for the certificate. So I had to walk across the street an extra time and get a gas station money order. Substitute powers, activate!

One of the two districts for which I wanted to work required a couple hours of training. The other district didn't give a fuck. The couple hours of training were pretty informative because the seasoned substitute coordinator, an uncouth older lady, laid all the information out there: Pack a bag of bullshit games in case you can't understand the teacher's lesson (or if the teacher didn't leave a lesson), maintain thick skin, never show weakness, send students to the principal's office with extreme prejudice, don't try to do more than you're supposed to do, don't share big ideas, shut the fuck up, get paid, go home, and enjoy your life. Some blonde newbie raised her hand, and asked, "Do we get paid for training today?" I rolled my eyes hard before our deadpan mentor answered, "This isn't a real job with paid training. There are no benefits other than it's easy and you're paid to do nothing."

That night I made my profile on the state's website where all the districts managed substitute requests, and selected that I would like morning phone calls in addition to the ability to claim jobs online. After looking over all the available jobs, I thought, "Nah. I'll start in a couple days." The next day I got about 30 calls. Holy shit. My phone never stopped vibrating. "OK. I'll start today."

Everything went down the way the old lady said it would. I would either claim jobs the night before via web or in the morning via phone. I'd show up at whichever school requested me, pick up my badge and time sheet at the front desk, babysit a class, drop off my badge and time sheet, and go home. Every other Friday the two districts for which I worked would directly deposit my income. The pay rate was the same $18 an hour slap-in-the-face I always got anywhere I worked, but felt like less because when my job offered the ability to click yes or no whether I wanted to come in or not I surprisingly (even under the threat of rape) clicked no too much. But there was always a job if I wanted one. P.E. jobs were the best jobs. No matter which grade or what plans the teacher left behind, I just let the students play dodge-ball and they were grateful. I have never before or after received the same immense respect I felt when young athletes spent the day calling me "coach."

Only once was P.E. a downer, and that was when I didn't realize I singed up for adaptive P.E. This is where I let students with profound mental disabilities play with balloons or scoot around on those square-seated skateboards. I was touched by the students' enthusiasm, but left a little heartbroken for bemoaning my own problems. I was born healthy, and so none of my problems were unsolvable. Life isn't fair doesn't mean what most of us who utter that phrase from time-to-time think it means. Life isn't fair, but I woke up healthy and with opportunities. Thanks to those children, I decided I was gong to try not to complain as much about dumb and insignificant setbacks.

I did such a good job at the very middle school I attended so many years ago, that the principal made me a permanent badge that hung with the other teachers' badges, and called me directly instead of offering up jobs through the online system. Principals were explicitly told not to do this, but most of them did anyway. Hey, a good sub is hard to come by! My only negative report came from an elementary school where I watched over a hybrid third and fourth grade class. Those little monsters were inconsolable, and so I ended the day having spaced their groupings of four desks into more traditional rows. Apparently some teachers don't like a substitute moving their shit (oh well, only a million other classrooms I could choose). I fondly remember the only time I taught kindergarten because a book I read challenged young readers to find visual absurdities in the illustrations like a bike with shoes instead of wheels. Those kindergartners would push and shove each other all over the reading rug trying to win a better chance at finding an undiscovered bird with a parachute (or whatever). I can't remember the last time I experienced such joy discovering a fish wearing a snorkel. I really didn't appreciate being a kid when I was one, but maybe I got bullied more than most. In other classes, I showed stacks of DVDs, and most days had at least an elective or planning period where I could mindlessly read on my phone or practice writing my last name on the board in impressive and dominating new ways.

Eventually, a principal clued me into a scam known as "charter schools" and said that with the very credentials I was already using to be a half-assed substitute teacher I could get a job as a half-assed full time teacher. Then, after just three short years (nine months with summers off), I could ascend to the same certificate status as teachers who studied education in college, and work full time in a district school. "This isn't even my final form!" I shouted, confusing the principal not privy to my inner monologue or possessing a basic understanding of power levels in anime. I hadn't solved my bad credit problem, but with the money from substitute teaching I was lurching closer to my goal of escaping Tammy. I decided I was going to become a real teacher and finally defeat her.

And by "defeat" I mean leave Tammy's house in the manner by which I left my hillbilly hellhole, which was stealthily and when nobody was looking.

I GET IT ALL BACK BETTER THAN BEFORE

Part 11

I go to the state's education career fair

As Arizona got more desperate for teachers the advertising for teaching jobs and benefits got proportionally louder and larger. I heard about the state's Department of Education Career Fair from a variety of sources, and signed up immediately. The event was in a midtown hotel, not even a good venue for something associated with the state, but there were three hallways of tables, plenty of people with whom to talk, and lots of swag. Lots and lots of swag. I filled up two bags with pens, magnets, stress balls, visors, toys, cellphone grips, notepads, and other freebies I would ultimately decide I didn't need and throw away. But in the moment, I felt like I won a supermarket sweepstakes and I needed to grab the most stuff before the buzzer. In addition to loot, there were plenty of scams. The district schools and charter schools not only needed teachers, but also instructional aides and support workers. I kept getting roped into conversations about how great an opportunity I'd be accepting if I agreed to be a low paid special education aide now with the possibility of career growth in the years to come. No thanks, get out of here with that bait and switch. I was on a mission to become a teacher.

After going down all the hallways, I was becoming discouraged that I hadn't really given my resume out to as many charter schools as I had hoped. Even though a teacher doesn't need to be certified to work in a charter school, most the charter school representatives still asked if I was certified. I told them no, but tried to convince them that my journalism major, history minor, and extensive experience working with children and adolescents left me more than qualified to teach English and History. Even though my pitch was convincing, I learned Language Arts and Social Studies weren't as in demand as Math and Science. I mean, think about it, mathematics is precise, but writing is subjective. A math teacher needs to know how to teach skills correctly so that every student solving a problem arrives at the same answer. A writing teacher can just wax poetic about creativity, grade subjectively, and praise whatever gets submitted. Eventually, on my way out, I came across an interesting table that offered a unique concept, a company that was both a behavioral health provider and a charter school. Students with behavior problems could earn credits and receive mental health counseling at the same time.

"I do not want to be considered for a behavioral health job." I said to one of the two representatives working the table at this combination charter school and behavior clinic as I handed over my resume. "I want to be a teacher."

"Trust us, we have openings for both an English teacher and a History teacher." Said the neatly dressed woman who accepted my resume then handed it to her neatly dressed male colleague. "Somebody will be in touch with you by phone for an interview."

The next day, I eagerly answered the phone on the first ring, but my excitement was doused as soon as the voice on the other end said, "Hi Jason! I'm calling because our job fair staff said you were interested in a job in behavioral health."

They bait and switched me! I tried to argue that I was intended for teaching English or History in the coming school year, but the person with whom I was speaking assured me both those teaching positions had been filled immediately in the early hours of the career fair. The person roped me into a conversation about how great an opportunity I'd be accepting if I agreed to start as a low paid behavioral health technician now with the possibility of career growth in the years to come. Although I was on a mission to become a teacher, I was also downtrodden and willing to schedule an interview for a job I wasn't at all interested in working.

When I showed up a couple days later, on a day I didn't accept any substitute gigs, I was interviewed by two very different women. There was a sweet grandmotherly type who knew a lot about counseling and trauma informed care, and a young business type who didn't say much, but looked angry for no reason. The grandmother spoke very kindly to me, and when I opened with, "I'm just a substitute…" She interrupted and made me say, "I'm not just a substitute." Her bedside manner was warm and validating, so I leveled with her that the job fair experience was disappointing except for the free loot. She laughed, and told me I should always follow my passions no matter what. The businesswoman tried to get the interview back on track every now and again, and obviously I wowed both of them with my extensive knowledge of the mental and behavioral healthcare system.

"We want to hire you!" was their conclusion.

"And this job will directly lead to teaching?" was my concern.

"Yeah, sure," went the bait and switch.

$18 an hour went the offer.

Part 12

I get rescued by Mexican coworkers

My new company was called Esperanza Siempre. Well, obviously this is a book where the names and places are tweaked to obfuscate their identity, but my new company was called something ridiculous in Spanish. So for the purpose of giving my job a name in this book, I picked "Always Hope" and wrote it in Spanish. Isn't it funny how counseling places selling self empowerment always call themselves something pseudo-inspirational? In my experience, what most clients need are direct cash payments. Sure, counseling has its place, but the members of my community are impoverished, without hope, and direct cash payments would resolve two thirds of their challenges. But instead they go to places called Esperanza Siempre and talk to counselors for an hour so business people can bill health insurance. Does it do any good? Who knows.

I accepted a job I didn't really want because by now I had located an apartment complex willing to overlook my credit problems. I wasn't moved in yet, but I was aware of my ability to move if I could afford the penalties associated with said credit problems. The apartment complex wasn't sprawling like my past place in the foothills, but smaller and built by brick in the 1970's. I was worried about the location and surrounding crime, but so far after what felt like hundreds of rejections its leasing office was the only property management to offer me a lifeline from Tammy. I was to pay both the first and last month's rent, a triple sized security deposit, and an additional payment to waive the credit check. To make that total payment I was going to need income more steady than substitute teaching. And I also naively thought there might be truth to being told I could eventually move over to the teaching side of the business.

Esperanza Siempre had gone through some changes between the short time since my interview and my first day. The nice grandmotherly lady was unceremoniously cast out, and the businesswoman without empathy was the de facto leader of the behavioral health side of the organization. She moved the clinic into a newly renovated building across the street from the affiliated high school and into the same parking lot as the affiliated middle school. I was sad to no longer be reporting to the grandma with empathy, but the businesswoman soon disappeared from the daily lives of us employees. Businesswoman's interests were luncheons, corporate meetings, travel for the sake of traveling, talking to the media, hiring people simply to grow the staff (several people had nothing to do all day), and doing sketchy shit with grants. For example, she kept accepting money for the purpose of helping homeless teenagers. Now, for all its problems, Arizona doesn't exactly have a pervasive homeless teenager problem. So the quota for helping 500 homeless teenagers was always unobtainable. In the whole time I worked at Esperanza Siempre we only ever met one legitimately homeless teenager.

My job was to teach life skills to juvenile probationers. The job was cushy because the teens sent to Esperanza Siempre by their probation officers were almost always polite because they needed us to provide positive reports to their judges. Our building was also set up like a recreation center, and none of us were real counselors. My upstairs office had three windows, several computer monitors, video games, my desk and a table. I had to tell businesswoman to stop adding computer monitors to my office because I had no use for them, but because she wanted everything to look modern and flashy I'd have to figure out what to do with each month's new monitor. I randomly mounted additional monitors to the wall and let them display news crawls or ocean waves all day. Our downstairs had a movie theater, a kitchen, a laundry room (for those non-existent homeless teenagers), and a pool hall. There were plenty of days where we just shot pool.

Another perk of Esperanza Siempre was that all my coworkers were Mexican, and loved taking care of me, feeding me, and supporting me. I would be in the middle of a session with a client in my office, and they would barge in with hot food. So my client and I would stop and eat tamales, fajitas, barbacoa or whatever other goodies I had coming to me that day courtesy of my very generous Mexican coworkers. There was the Old Alpha Male coworker who brought in the only legitimate business. He was a retired probation officer, and through his court contacts we received a steady stream of referrals. Without Old Alpha Male, our business was only the sham grants fraudulently solicited by Businesswoman. There was a former probationer, still a teen, who now worked in our bike shop. The idea behind the bike shop was that thanks to a deal with the transportation department, we would receive all the unclaimed bicycles left on busses. Bike Shop Teen would then refurbish them with probationers who earned some kind of mechanic's certificate. The bikes would then become charitable donations to foster care or sold to reinvest into our youth programs. Bike Shop Teen immediately gifted me a nice bike with solid rubber tires. We later discovered that he mostly stole inventory and sold it for personal profit. Until I helped bring over a former coworker from my now smoldering group home company, I was the only white person. My Group Home Buddy arrived all fired up to help homeless teens, and was surprised to find out we didn't know any. He struggled with sitting around getting paid to do nothing, but I enjoyed the leisurely days. And the free tacos!

Most importantly, I worked with an Old Alpha Female coworker who should have been in the position occupied by Businesswoman. If she were in charge, the clinic could have really been a force for good in the lives of teenagers (homeless or otherwise). Instead, she was propped up as an assistant to Businesswoman and made to be the randomized department director many times over for however many sham grants arrived. She became increasingly overwhelmed by the absurdity of the grants for which she was supposed to respond with business solutions. Just imagine driving around trying to find homeless teenagers! Eventually she went crazy and just made herself the honorary lunch lady, and cooked food in the kitchen for us and the probationers here for life skills counseling. One day I opened up to Old Alpha Female about my abusive living situation, and how I was having coerced sex every night under the threat of being homeless. She responded by coming into my office an hour later with a rubber banded roll of hundred dollar bills amounting to what I needed to rent my own apartment.

In absolute disbelief, I thanked her profusely and promised to pay her back (and I eventually finished paying her back). She told me to leave right then and there, and go reserve an apartment in that little brick complex built in the 1970's. I flew down the street at felony speeds, and leased an upstairs apartment that would be ready in a couple of weeks. I've never before or after had coworkers like my Mexican family.

Part 13

I travel to Chicago for counseling certification

How could a fake behavioral health clinic with no real counselors stay in business? The short answer was that it could not stay in business. This is really weird, but I'll try to explain. Even with the charter middle and high schools, Esperanza Siempre wasn't profitable, and thus in the hole for a couple million dollars. The recently deceased CEO was apparently friends with the CEO of one of the more legitimate (but still sketchy) adult mental health clinics, and they had some sort of Freemasonry-style pact to not let each other's legacy wither and die. So the CEO of the adult mental health clinic bought and absorbed Esperanza Siempre, and intended to let it continue existing without interference. But while that deal was happening, the state's Regional Behavioral Health Authority changed and things got a little more complicated. I could take more paragraphs to properly explain, but I could also leave a sentence saying "health insurance gobbledygook" and the point would have been made. Under the new rules, networks were pressured not to be children exclusive or adult exclusive providers. So places that previously only served children needed to add adult services, and places that previously only served adults needed to add children services. The adult organization that bought Esperanza Siempre had already started building a children's program which left a little uncertainty about what to do with us.

Funny enough, I had once participated in building that children's program and that is where I originally met Tammy. So while an employee of Esperanza Siempre, I was always a little uncomfortable when we had anything to do with the fledgling children's services over in our parent company's side of things. Predictably, the higher ups eventually realized that simultaneously running both a new, but legitimate, children's clinic with real counselors, a couple psychiatric doctors, and an established brand, and, a fake clinic of no real value, sandwiched between a charter middle and high school, at the same time made no sense. They decided to let the real children's clinic absorb us. The director of the real children's clinic, identical to my businesswoman boss in every way except she was white, was chomping at the bit. She was doing a shitty job of growing her new children's clinic, and really wanted access to Old Alpha Male's probation contacts. Our own evil businesswoman had almost lost this battle to stay our own entity until her Caucasian counterpart got leukemia. The real children's clinic losing its director to a yearlong recovery bought us about twelve months to carve out a separate business identity. Businesswoman decided we were going to become a boutique substance abuse clinic for teens.

"Jason," Businesswoman began trepidatiously, "You're the most academically minded staff so I need you to travel to Chicago and attend this prestigious substance abuse counselor certification program. Success in this endeavor is very important to the longevity of Esperanza Siempre. If all of you can become certified substance abuse counselors, that bitch won't be able to beat leukemia and become our boss. You're going to go first, and then help everyone else."

I was on board because I hadn't been anywhere by plane since I was young enough that my parents were taking me on their vacations, and Businesswoman provided me an enormous food budget. Enormous like I would expend actual effort trying to spend all the money. The money was, of course, siphoned from the grant to help homeless teenagers. I had to take a pre-test to even qualify for the training, but with the help of the Internet I scored 100 percent. Since therapists from all over the country were converging in Chicago, I figured I'd best represent Arizona by shaving a mustache and wearing a cowboy hat. And believe you me, I felt like a bad ass at the airport, a bad ass on the plane, and a bad ass at the hotel. But for some reason as soon as I was seated in the training hall I felt like a huge dork. Go figure.

In addition to feeling embarrassment because I had a mustache and a cowboy hat, a sense of dread consumed me when I learned just how rigorous this damn certification was going to be to complete. Not only was I going to need to train for two weeks, I was going to have to spend a year recording client sessions, sending the audio back to a curriculum supervisor, earn passing grades on a fuck ton of skills, and continue participating in monthly remote training. I realized I may have to get back to Arizona and start looking for another job, because this shit I signed up for seemed maddeningly difficult. With the comfort in knowing I'd just bail on Businesswoman and Esperanza Siempre, I enjoyed the rest of the training. The instructors were big on role plays, and in one lesson they paired me with a Jamaican lady who spoke with a heavy accent. When the instructors asked us to switch roles I thought I'd be funny and suddenly adopt her Creole Caribbean dialect. Oops! The audience did not perceive that as anything but culturally insensitive, with the offense exacerbated by my mustache and cowboy hat.

Near the end of the training, I actually learned a lot about recovery from substance use and abuse. I also learned that the recovery techniques had value beyond substance use, because we were taught to think of substance use as a negative behavior like other negative behaviors such as lying, stealing, anger, etc. There's nothing you can say to make somebody want to stop using, but if you can tease out their positive personal goals and help them become successful then a return to using will naturally feel less appealing. This stuff made sense. The stages of change, the functional analysis, the problem solving, the healthy communication, the prosocial replacement activity, the safety plans, the accountability partners, the feelings thermometer, the happiness inventory, goal setting and follow through, short term rewards or consequences, triggers, coping skills, risk environments, and natural supports. In a night near the end of my stay, I reflected on all the material I had learned, how knowing all this would have made me a better group home supervisor, and how I wouldn't be here if not for my Mexican family back at Esperanza Siempre. Everybody at work I cared about was still counting on me to avoid a hostile takeover from the real children's clinic. I also admired my hotel room, and the peace that came from not being raped by Tammy. Right then and there I decided that when my little brick apartment was ready for me I was going to furnish it exactly like this quiet and cozy hotel room. And since I had my Mexican family to thank for my coming freedom, I decided I could complete these certification requirements for them and save our independent agency.

Even with the audio recording requirement, I earned both my basic and advanced certifications in less than six months.

Part 14

I have the best job of my life

Old Alpha Female helped me move out of Tammy's house the weekend Tammy and her daughter went to Phoenix for a softball tournament. We only needed one trip with the small hauler I rented, and there was enough time to neatly clean out the room and say goodbye to the dog. I had gotten my apartment keys earlier in the week, and already stashed toiletries, food, and, of course, mucha cerveza. Lots of beer. Old Alpha Female gifted me a mini-dryer, and I fulfilled my dream of setting up an efficiency apartment almost identical to my hotel room during substance abuse certification training. I met my neighbor when I carried up another box of belongings, and again worried about possible crime in my new location because the young man had tattoos all over his face. But not wanting to get off on the wrong foot, I introduced myself and we exchanged pleasantries. When I told him I worked at Esperanza Siempre, his demeanor turned much friendlier, and he told me Old Alpha Male was once his probation officer and really supported him. When I found out my new neighbor had several little kids, I gifted him an equal number of bikes assembled by Bike Shop Teen. My connection to Esperanza Siempre was the gift that kept on giving. I was definitely not going to have a repeat of the Hillbilly situation with any of my new neighbors. Plus, the bricks made it hard for all of us to even hear each other through the walls.

Tammy coming home and discovering me gone was hilarious. I got several text messages from her feigning surprise and concern, and I just breadcrumbed little answers about being time to move out because I was back on my feet. She didn't take long to ask if I wanted to drop her my address so she could come by and help christen my new place, and while at first I resisted she later guilted me into telling her where I lived because apparently her teen was attached to me. They did come for a visit, and the chit chat was calm enough. I could tell Tammy was secretly seething because she made snide comments about how soon would it be before I got some hoes. I mostly ignored her, and drew pictures with her daughter. They left, and Tammy never came back. She tried to entice me into accepting some booty calls, but I invented a game to offer up new excuses with each excuse sounding more and more ridiculous. When I told her I couldn't come because I was in line for a superhero movie in full costume, she went off on me and argued that I dumped her after she provided me a home. Finally, I unloaded on her for being a psycho rapist bitch then blocked her number. To date, I've had no further communication with Tammy.

The weeks at work flew by because I loved my job. There was no difference in enjoyment between a Monday or a Friday at Esperanza Siempre. My job was already great before substance abuse counseling certification, but even better after we were legitimate. My primary responsibility became the Intensive Outpatient Program, or IOP, which was three weekly three hour classes. That's nine hours of court ordered drug counseling our juvenile probationers had to attend a week. Obviously we filled a lot of that time with pizza, pool and movies, but since I was certified we were able to offer a lot of curriculum, too. Esperanza Siempre made so much money on the IOP, I wasn't really expected to do much with my other 31 hours a week. Yes, my income was still terrible, but my core responsibility was nine hours of IOP. Technically all the teens attending IOP had either me or Old Alpha Male assigned as an individual counselor, but nobody really prioritized the individual appointments. The teens were in school during the day anyway, and IOP was in the evenings. Some weeks I would literally only go in for IOP, and otherwise just live my awesome life.

I also enjoyed the respect I received as an expert in my field. Probation officers, lawyers, judges, and even the principals of our two affiliated charter schools all consulted with me about teenage drug use. I would even visit the schools to support sobriety programs and offer additional education on the topic. Businesswoman, in another effort to elevate Esperanza Siempre above the real children's clinic, sent me and Old Alpha Male to the Pima County Health Department to get certified in a Latino version of Sex Education. We mostly joked about our name card pronouns (OK, look, this was the first time we knew pronouns could be sensitive), but graduated and started teaching sex ed, too. Businesswoman, for all her fraud and abuse, made some smart moves because of her rivalry with the director of the real children's clinic. Esperanza Siempre collected enough niche programs that there was no more threat of being acquired and stripped for parts. Old Alpha Male and I really did make a great team. He was the big dog with all the contacts whom the teens loved. The Hispanic teens especially looked up to him as an older Hispanic male. And I was the academically minded younger guy who could inject curriculum at the appropriate moments. Old Alpha Male and I grew so close that Old Alpha Male decided to put off his retirement by another five years. Our gig was too easy, fun and lucrative to give up. Lucrative, but, I was accidentally cursed with knowledge that while I was only making $18 an hour, Businesswoman charged almost $40 an hour for my certified counseling. But getting paid $18 an hour for 40 hours a week when you really only work nine is OK. Group Home Buddy finally got the hang of ignoring the homeless teen mandate, and offered cool services to our probationers like helping them mix their original rap songs. Experts or not we just did stuff to edify teens.

The last amenity that made Esperanza Siempre the best job of my life was the opening of a popular chicken restaurant next door. For the longest time in its construction, a teasing sign on the door said "Opening in Two Weeks" but then nothing ever happened. Every assumed second week I would walk over there, pull the handle, and be disappointed to discover the establishment locked. When I peered through the glass, everything appeared to be finished. Then one day, I pulled hard and the door flung open. My heart froze in shock, but then I saw a group of men in suits standing around staring at me. An old bald guy everyone else had just been listening to turned to me and said, "Hey, sorry, this is a corporate meeting, but the restaurant will be open in two weeks." Several two weeks later, the popular chicken restaurant opened next door to Esperanza Siempre, and gave me a permanent lunch spot. On so many days, we would walk over there the whole group of us: Me, Old Alpha Male, Old Alpha Female, Group Home Buddy, and Bike Shop Teen. Esperanza Siempre was the best job of my life.

Part 15

I notice pandemic paranoia

I don't know if I'm clairvoyant or just pessimistic, but I knew COVID-19 was going to be bad the first time I saw it in the news. I don't do my backwards research for this book, everything as I remember it is from the top of my head, but I recall first reading about the situation in Wuhan, and thinking, "This is going to affect the entire world." I also figured Trump making COVID political, racist, and worse than if he did nothing was a given. The wet markets in the globe's poorest locations no doubt exist in a feedback loop following overconsumption of resources in the globe's wealthiest locations. COVID is simultaneously the fault of all of us and none of us.

Life at Esperanza Siempre knocked about as always. I'd roll into work at some time close to IOP, and spend the minutes to showtime just chilling with the boys Old Alpha Male, Group Home Buddy, and Bike Shop Teen. I'd ask if they had seen the news, and they were loosely aware of COVID, but they had a fleeting interest in thinking about the other side of the world longer than needed to get back into a discussion about sports. When the first case hit America, and the CDC started dropping information like older people needed to be more careful, Old Alpha Male took the path of, "Whatever happens to me, happens to me. I accept my fate." This remained his response throughout our early conversations about maybe introducing some mitigating strategies.

Soon, out of a sense of duty, I started incorporating lessons about COVID into IOP. The probationers mostly laughed at me, and two of them invented a new greeting where they directly spit into each other's hands before shaking them and fist bumping. Even before COVID, I affectionately called our boys on probation "dumb criminals." Most of them were on probation because they smoked marijuana at school and got caught. Pro tip, schools are federal property so school is one of the dumbest places to smoke. Even getting caught across the street would make a world of difference. Often times sympathetic police officers would charge our boys with paraphernalia, not wanting to saddle them with a felony. Unless our boys were rude then police officers threw the book at them.

The girls on probation, on the other hand, were not dumb criminals. In my experience, boys and girls use drugs for different reasons. The Girls IOP was full of sex trafficking cases, suicidal and homicidal ideation, and a whole other spectrum of mental disorders. Maybe I should have mentioned earlier that IOP was actually two IOPs, but the Boys IOP was our main service, our booming business, and the reason Esperanza Siempre was able to stay afloat. The Girls IOP was a little offshoot less than a quarter in size that ran simultaneously upstairs. The female counselor that was hired to run the Girls IOP was a strange hippie lady who described herself as a suicide survivor, and decorated her office with photos of jumpers on 9/11. She taught that suicide feels like needing to jump out of a burning building because there is no other choice. I don't know how I felt about that, but didn't think the messaging was right for a substance abuse class. Strange Hippie Lady also irked us downstairs because she didn't enforce the dress code. We were strict on things like marijuana socks, shirts that referenced being high or faded, and, you know, generally beer logos and contraband that didn't belong in IOP.

Strange Hippie Lady had no will to enforce rules, so her girls showed up half naked and ran wild. A contentious staff meeting settled that Strange Hippie Lady wasn't allowed to facilitate breaks at the same time as us, because the behavior of the girls negatively impacted the behavior of the boys. My opinion was that it didn't have to be that way, and the girls were just as capable of behaving as the boys. In fact, everything went much smoother in the random nights I covered Girls IOP. Funny how kids test boundaries because structure and routine is comforting. Because Strange Hippie Lady came to us with a Master's degree in trauma therapy, she was selected as the one who would complete the same certification training as me, but then continue and get certified in the supervisory version of the curriculum. The idea being that when she finished, additional staff would no longer need to travel to Chicago for certification, and the new hires would just train under Strange Hippie Lady. That sounded like a nightmare for those poor future staff I'd never meet, and ironically Strange Hippie Lady moved through the certification requirements much slower than I did. I'll concede she was a better individual counselor, but my rapport building and genuine relationships made for better audio recordings.

What I did like about Strange Hippie Lady is that she took COVID seriously. When I was still noticing the percolating pandemic paranoia, Strange Hippie Lady was already on top of bringing in hand sanitizer, spacing out chairs, and adding tape to the floor to encourage social distancing. When masks started appearing in public, Strange Hippie Lady was an early adopter who wore a mask around the office. I didn't have to be the first, but I could follow suit and not feel awkward around Old Alpha Male and our probationers. When the public started hoarding toilet paper, Old Alpha Male and I emptied both the upstairs and downstairs women's restrooms and moved that supply into our own homes. We did this mostly for laughs, and not because we thought we would run out of toilet paper. When pandemic paranoia came to a boil, the staff of Esperanza Siempre did come together and acknowledge that our drug counseling and life skills services needed to adapt. The only obstacle was that Businesswoman liked the opulence in her life (remember the travel and lunches), and wasn't about to let something like a global pandemic ruin her fun scamming health insurance and ripping off grants.

I… COVID-19

Part 16

I watch my boss turn into Trump

Businesswoman felt threatened in every gathering where we brought up COVID-19, so she started making bizarre moves like splitting our traditional team meeting in half and holding separate meetings for clinical staff (me, Old Alpha Male, and Strange Hippie Lady) and non-clinical staff (Old Alpha Female, Bike Shop Teen, and Group Home Buddy). She did whatever she could to silence the majority opinion that we needed to respond to COVID. Whenever Strange Hippie Lady laid tape on the floor, Businesswoman was right behind her to peel it off. Whenever a big COVID event hit the news, Businesswoman was quick to point out the incident was a state, a county, or a town away from us. At some point, she completely broke from reality and just retreated to her office to forward ultra right-wing propaganda emails. When our affiliated charter middle and high schools started having confirmed exposures, and asking classrooms to stay home and quarantine, Businesswoman actively gas-lighted us that reports from the schools were false. She pushed back that the two schools had nothing to do with us, and under no circumstance would we ever be working from home. When the public discourse coined the term "essential businesses" Businesswoman decided the matter was settled, and we had a duty to carry on as we had always.

Businesswoman reconvened her clinical staff and non-clinical staff (a distinction that had never before mattered) just once to teach some crap she downloaded called the Wisdom of Geese. She taught that geese fly in a V-formation with ease, but as soon as one goose drops out of formation the whole team has to expend that much more energy to propel forward. I guess she thought we would pull together in ignoring the threat of COVID, but instead we all cracked jokes and she became irate. Later she threw herself a birthday party, and made the gathering a potluck since that would throw up the most hurdles against social distancing and cross contamination (Good job, you got us). Finally, the local ordinances responded enough to the pandemic that we had to recognize COVID or risk a surprise inspection and possible shutdown. By now, I had already recorded a series of substance abuse videos and uploaded them to several social media sites under some version of "Esperanza Siempre Boys IOP." Businesswoman found out, admired the high view count, and tried to take credit. She also demanded all the passwords to my sites. When I didn't give her the passwords, she hired a new social media manager and asked this person to recreate my work. Obviously Businesswoman's power grab failed spectacularly, but not through any fault of the new social media manager. I liked Social Media Manager, she was nice, but, like Group Home Buddy before her, she had to adjust to our simple life where nobody's job had real meaning. As long as IOP happened, everything else was extra.

Now firmly in the time of COVID, we moved IOP online. This conversion went OK, and once again my expertise was required to save the agency. I figured out how to make our curriculum interactively digital, how to offer the groups in video conferencing apps, and how to streamline sending the mass invites to all probationers' phones and email addresses. I also handled moderator duties in the live video, but we didn't have to deal with too many behaviors from the boys. Remember, they still wanted positive reports for their court hearings. Sometimes boys would sign on showing stacks of cash, drug paraphernalia, or some sex related nonsense, but they quickly acquiesced to following the same rules they followed in person. As expected, Girls IOP was a dud. Strange Hippie Lady lacked the onscreen charisma of me and Old Alpha Male. The referrals from probation started specifically asking for our popular "Virtual IOP" and for a stretch of time we had an enjoyable new normal. Even Old Alpha Female and Group Home Buddy found a new sense of purpose, and recorded a lot of original content. Group Home Buddy broadcast videos of all the life skills he used to teach transitional-age-youth in our last job. With Businesswoman buying whatever tech I requested, we were able to quickly improve scripts, production values and post-editing. Sometimes I asked Businesswoman to buy shit I just wanted to take home and own. She was dumb about technology, but enjoyed feeling like she was steering this ship through a storm.

We converted our services to the web as quickly as we did because staff met in secret on the far side of the recently closed chicken restaurant. That was how we circumvented Businesswoman turning into Trump. When Businesswoman was telling us not to dare call families and cancel IOP, we met in secret and decided to do exactly that. When Businesswoman wanted us to call the courts and let the probation officers and lawyers know we were still open for in-person meetings, we met in secret and confirmed we would tell agency partners and customers to use video conferencing apps. When the county finally left Businesswoman no choice, she just assumed that we accomplished everything in the same hour she made her announcement. What an idiot. I was proud of my Mexican family for holding those secret parking lot meetings. Even Social Media Manager, who hadn't been with us very long, was willing to go on strike if the county hadn't forced Businesswoman's hand. Now our only remaining objective was the ability to work from home.

Part 17

I get fired for quitting

Working from home was a hard fought battle, won only because we went to the parent company's HR office. We submitted formal requests to work from home backed by miscellaneous documentation. If we shared we were concerned about infirm family members or if we ourselves had comorbidities then our parent company would begrudgingly issue short term work-from-home plans. Businesswoman went nuts, and searched for more ways to act like a psycho. First, she scheduled individual supervisions over video, something she had never done before. In fact, she had never observed a single IOP, listened to any of my session audio, or provided any feedback on my job performance whatsoever. But now she scheduled little punishment sessions where we had to appear on video for her to confirm we weren't wearing pajamas. Second, she wrote a lot of new policy during this work-from-home time, and created new forms she wanted us to fill out for targeting daily, weekly and monthly goals. Obviously we adapted quickly and found efficient ways to defeat her forms, but I knew in the back of my mind that Businesswoman was going to keep innovating new ways to act like a psycho until she found the weapon to dismantle our contentness.

The first time Trump prematurely declared COVID-19 was about to disappear from our lives, Businesswoman released her ridiculous timetable for us to return to the office and welcome back in-person services. Even though I predicted she would have to scrap her plans, I applied for other jobs just in case she succeeded. While drinking a beer in one hand, and swiping on jobs in the other hand, I watched TV and applied for anything that had to do with teaching so long as there was the easy apply button. If the job posting redirected to an offsite application then I mentally wrote off that job. I reflected on how joining Esperanza Siempre had been an unwelcome detour toward becoming a teacher, but somehow became the best job of my life. Well, best job before COVID. Now that my resume boasted certified substance abuse counseling, lots more schools were interested in me. Before long, I had a phone interview with a charter school company looking to hire multiple teachers for the next academic year.

The speed with which the charter school company hired me blew my mind. The HR lady sent me some sample curriculum, detailed student grading, and other spreadsheets before I accepted a call from a panel interview. The interviewers included the same HR lady, a superintendent, an assistant superintendent, and two principals from two of the five schools belonging to this charter school company. The panel verified that I understood how to interpret test scores and grade point averages, asked me to speed run through teaching that sample curriculum, thanked me for my time, then sent me an offer letter about as quickly as we hung up. I was over the moon happy to have finally reached my goal of becoming a full time teacher; a full time teacher on the condition that COVID didn't surge and spoil the year. So now I felt pretty confident that no matter what happened at Esperanza Siempre or my new school I would at least be employed somewhere. With the whole summer ahead, I picked a date I thought would give the school enough time to replace me if I stayed with the IOP, and I rode things out at Esperanza Siempre before deciding to leave or not.

Businesswoman said something triggering over the phone almost immediately after I gained the confidence to talk back to her, so I gloated, "Consider this my 90 day's notice. Coming this Fall, ya boy is a teacher!" I felt pretty smug, but she became enraged and fired me for quitting. She also called back with the audacity to ask that I drive from my apartment to the office to return my work issued laptop and smartphone. I gloated again, "That's your problem to solve. Everything is going to be on my porch in a box!" I wiped the hard drives on both the phone and computer, and tossed each device outside. She sent some maintenance person from our parent company to come collect the gear, and that was the end of my employment at Esperanza Siempre. I felt guilty knowing Old Alpha Male would struggle to keep Virtual IOP going without me managing the technical side of things, but also felt relief that I didn't have to work again until school started. If it started.

"Would I qualify for unemployment?" I wondered, a couple beers deep into celebrating my liberation from Businesswoman's right-wing lunacy. By now, my friends at Esperanza Siempre had already reached out with their condolences, friendly ribbing, and best wishes. Also by now, I knew Businesswoman had reported to HR that her reasons (plural) for firing me included gloating about a new job, and forcing my coworkers and clients to view pornography. What? Malware infected one of our social media accounts not managed by me and displayed pornography for a hilariously awkward amount of time. Businesswoman, with impressive dishonesty or unbelievable paranoia, now blamed me for the sex images all over one of her abandoned attempts at online outreach. When I wrote my unemployment claim I included a technical paragraph in case the government worker reading about my firing understood malware, and I included a layman's paragraph in case the government worker reading about my firing never heard of malware. Still, I figured getting terminated for "forcing my coworkers and clients to view pornography" was going to prevent me from receiving assistance. For the first month of staying home, I tightened my belt and lived very frugally. There were still three months until school started (if school started), and my money needed to last. Then one day, on my birthday to be exact, Arizona approved my federally enhanced unemployment claim, and deposited a huge sum in my bank account. The total amount was backdated to the date of my claim, and I was to receive another $800 every next week. Fuck yes! Fuck you, Businesswoman! Ka-fucking-ching!

Part 18

I live my best life on unemployment

I never vacationed worry-free for months on end before. Sure, there were times I was unemployed after rage quitting a job, but the ecstasy never outlived the panic to find the next $18 an hour abusive situation. Getting paid to stay home was an eye opener. Life could be amazing for all of us with a universal basic income. There's no reason for all of us to work when computers can do so many tasks on our behalf. The only reason any $18 an hour job exists is to rape the planet out of existence so asshole billionaires can own extra yachts and private jets. COVID-19 brought to light that our lives exist in a misery machine that rich people could have switched off at any time. I personally have never been happier or felt more fulfilled than when I got paid to stay home. I was free to sleep when I wanted, eat and drink when I wanted, poop when I wanted, work on hobby projects and be creative when I wanted, and just exist without a sense of existential dread.

Something I never did was order food from the delivery apps. I just couldn't. When I supervised my group home, a hygiene challenged teenager with a beater vehicle used all the delivery apps to make money. The jalopy he drove to transport food for customers was absolutely disgusting. Just packed with filth. Even though I admired his hustle, I wouldn't want to eat anything he moved inside his smelly car. About once a week I would mask up and walk to the grocery store. This was my main form of exercise. I would walk to the grocery store then challenge myself to carry back heavier and heavier items. I also never before cooked so much at home. I bought a cast iron skillet, and lived off burgers and steaks. I guess that qualified as cooking. I also bought a blender, and mixed many flavorful margaritas and piña coladas. Assured that the next $800 was always a week away, and with more good food and drink than I could consume, I happily settled into an astronaut's sleep schedule and did my part to slow the spread. I watched everything the main streaming services had to offer, including movies from foreign libraries.

I did not date during this time. I also hadn't dated during my housing and employment crisis. There wasn't a good way to date while living with my Jewish landlady and the fattest man alive or a good way to date while living with Tammy or a good way to date while getting my substance abuse counseling certification. Living in my peaceful brick apartment would have been a great time to start socializing again, but now the world was afflicted with COVID. I didn't exactly feel lonely, even though I was alone 95 percent of the time, but re-downloaded the dating apps to start some conversations. Suspiciously, most the women with whom I connected weren't interested in simply being pen pals. Even though my profile said I was only seeking a chat buddy, I got hit with a lot of, "So are we ever going to meet or are you wasting my time?" I judged women who were so willing to thumb their noses at the pandemic. They would argue, "But do you have any symptoms? Neither do I so it's fine." I imagined this debate played out between thousands of other would-be couples like us, and hoped most would decide not to take the risk.

Then something wonderful happened. I met a stunning brunette named Sam who was also only seeking a chat buddy. Like me, she wanted to see the pandemic resolve as quickly and fully as possible, and saw dating as an unnecessary, maybe even selfish, risk. So we spent the summer getting to know each other over text and video. Sam started the morning tradition of pouring her coffee then calling me on video to watch the sunrise. She worked as a recruiter for a large company that ran charitable golf tournaments, and was involved with several neighborhood and non-profit projects. She was one of those very social and effective communicators who stayed busy working on complex initiatives that would improve the community. Her favorite animal was the bat. I've always liked people who can name a clear favorite animal. To take the time to reflect on all the wildlife, decide which one is the subjective best, and advocate for it through art and sharing, is something only a special person does. My coffee chats with Sam sustained my spirit throughout most of the COVID summer. Unfortunately, maybe because I was otherwise not talking to people, I forgot there are aspects of my personality I shouldn't share. I thought I went on a funny rant about how much I hate hillbillies, but a flip switched and Sam suddenly found me derogatory and unpleasant. I backpedaled to explain that I only meant my past upstairs neighbors, but the damage was done. No more sunrise coffee chats with Sam.

Losing my sunrise coffee chats with Sam caused me to feel the crushing weight of my solitude, so I decided to say "fuck it" and meet the next woman in person.

Part 19

I start meeting women from home

Swiping during the pandemic was ego boosting because I matched way more than ever before. I usually cast a wide net to capture matches several years older than me, but with sex-starved pandemic women I could streamline my search to my age and significantly younger. I matched with many college students which led to incredibly sexy conversations and an accumulation of seductive photos. Unfortunately, these conversations fizzled out fast when I said I wasn't willing to meet in the throes of COVID-19. I thought I was ready, but maybe I wasn't. I really just wanted to replace my sunrise coffee chats. The college aged women would insult me, accuse me of being gay, and then unmatch as quickly as they had sent their steamy media. I turned the age filter back up, and matched with two unique women: Scout and Kasumi.

Scout was a 40 year old woman whose body was stunning beyond words. I didn't get a good look at her face right away, because she sent two styles of pictures. She sent nudes with her head cropped off, and highly filtered face photos with animal ears. She spoke very disparagingly of herself, but I convinced her to send an unfiltered portrait. Turns out Scout was a normal, attractive woman! I suppose she was self-conscious of a crooked smile and wrinkles exacerbated by smoking, but nothing compared to what cigarettes had done to Tammy. I was really happy with Scout, and after she was comfortable with me we did lots of video chats. Unlike my sunrise coffee chats, Scout tended to call at night. She started our first video chat with a cigarette outside, then she propped her phone up in her bedroom and got naked on her mattress. She asked me, "Am I blowing your mind right now?"

Video calls from Scout became frequent, and I at times felt overwhelmed. If I just didn't answer, she'd text me to either ask when I would be available or if something was wrong. I wanted to stem back the video chats, but again Scout was nice and fulfilling a need. Scout was in a similar line of work as me (or at least when I'm employed), but still meeting with little children from her caseload. Despite COVID, she was still visiting in-person daycare and providing hands on behavior coaching. She said what she liked about me was that I was nice compared to the men that abuse her. What? Apparently she met up with lots of men who only wanted to have sex in their cars while parked on her street, and (surprise) that never led to anything meaningful. I couldn't climb inside Scout's head, but to me simply not meeting men like that would be an easy filter. Still, she constantly referred to herself as a "slut", and then footnoted that she hoped to meet somebody nice.

Finally, Scout pushed for an in-person meeting between us. She knew my hesitancy, and procured a negative COVID test in advance of my protestations. She wanted to come to my apartment, with which she was already familiar from video chatting, after she got off work the next Friday. She proposed a sleepover date at my place which should include baking me a cheesecake, wearing an outfit I would request in advance, and then staying up all night playing my old school video games. I mean, for real, that sounded like a hell of a deal. Scout was a dream, I just didn't want her bringing COVID into my life after I had successfully avoided infection for so long. Sure she was negative now, but that test is only as meaningful as the day it was printed. Scout still had to visit daycare until Friday. I guess because I liked the attention, I told her yes, with my home address forthcoming, watched her bake the cheesecake over video wearing just an apron, requested the sleepover outfit include a thong, and set little goals for our old school video game marathon. I did all this knowing I would wake up Friday morning and cancel. I did feel guilty leading her on, and guiltier yet when she told me she went shopping for a thong since she didn't normally wear them.

The morning I pulled the rug out from under Scout, I simply said I wasn't going to send her my address after all because I reconsidered her job duties and wasn't comfortable with the risk. She expressed disappointment, but not anger (that came later), and followed up with photos of her outfit which she modeled from a daycare bathroom. She did look hot as fuck. She also teased that I would not see the thong, and then later complained that she was even stuck wearing the thong (haha). Scout video called me that night as usual, just to chat as we normally would, but she peppered the conversation with questions about whether there was anything she could do to make me comfortable with the risk. She even proposed we could wear masks during our intended sleepover date. This is when I decided to engage in a lie that might turn me on. I decided to tell Scout that while I was scared of catching COVID, because she works with children and meets men in parking lots, the real reason I psyched myself out of letting her spend the night was because I was sexually inexperienced. In fact, I was still a virgin.

"What? That's not true!" Exclaimed Scout. She continued, in disbelief, "How is that possible?" My heart raced in our most recent video chat leading up to this moment. She showed me her breasts, rubbed them, and asked me what I would be doing if we were in the middle of our missed sleepover date. That's when I blurted out that I had never had sex before. She was stunned, asked her follow up questions, thought over my answers, then concluded, "Yes, I should have figured it out. I'm a sure thing, and no man who is sexually active would pass me up." I quizzically wondered if my feelings about not wanting to catch COVID were so unusual that no other man would choose risk avoidance, but I was also really hard from the waves of humiliation washing over me now that my sexy friend thought I was painfully unlaid. Scout got super reassuring, thanked me for being brave enough to tell her the truth, and insisted that she wanted to help me. I got really, really hard. Scout asked if I would show her my penis, and I obliged. She squealed over my "beautiful" erection. She told me I only lacked confidence and initiative. Scout was so compassionate about this embarrassing development that I felt guilty for lying to her. But also really, really, really hard.

I wanted to come clean to Scout, but the video chats continued and she double downed on sex coaching me. Scout said she would answer any question, so I submitted a series of absurd inquiries and always got off on her careful explanations. I asked if men having sex in porn yell "you're so hot" because the friction from thrusting continues to heat the women's vaginas (like starting a campfire by rubbing sticks together) to the point where they can no longer continue to avoid a burn. She told me, no, that couldn't happen due to natural lubrication. Ahhh. I asked if her vagina was sealed shut by default, and she had to consciously open and close it with her mind to urinate or allow penetration, and learned that, no, her vagina is lucid by default and can dilate when needed. Ahhh. I asked her if her vaginal wetness was more foamy like soap bubbles, slippery like baby oil, or thicker like petroleum jelly. None of the above. Ahhh. Scout was blessed with an abundance of patience, and always telling me she was willing to come and show me everything I wanted to know. She argued that she should be my first lover because my virginity would mean something to her. I assured her she was my first choice if the pandemic ever ended.

Scout finally proposed a compromise. She said my sexual education was imperative to her, and that she was sending me a sex toy. She was sending me a vagina sleeve. Scout said she would send me a male masturbator so I could experience a facsimile of sex, and then when the pandemic ended we would finally schedule our sleepover date. I would finally experience, as she put it, "the real thing." Scout and I had been video chatting for so long, and she was so sensitive toward me those last weeks as an out virgin, that I considered sending her my address. I never owned a pocket pussy before, and Scout wanting to buy it for me added a layer of lust toward the idea of trying one. I said fuck it, gave her my address, and thanked her for her generosity. Scout sent screenshots of the pleasurable purchase, and then over the next 24 hours sent updated tracking information. When she received the delivery confirmation, she waited with bated breath for an update. She told me to send pictures or video if I was comfortable doing so.

I'll admit I enjoyed the vagina sleeve more than expected. Vagina sleeves are amazing, and I became addicted to mine (but overuse and quitting like a fiend swearing off cocaine is another story). The vagina sleeve blew my mind, and I was genuinely grateful to Scout for bringing this treat into my life. I sent her a video of the inaugural voyage, and she remarked how happy this made her before a somewhat snide comment about how she wished I would allow her to participate. Before long, I started ordering condoms to use with my vagina sleeve because doing so made cleanup so much easier. Scout even warned me that I was spending too much time with my new toy, and she was becoming annoyed that I was no longer communicating interest in her taking my virginity. Eventually, the frequency of Scout's video calls noticeably dropped, and I sensed her pulling away from me. When she did finally call, I asked her what she had been up to and she singsongingly told me she had been dating a sweet hillbilly. What?

Scout told me she had been setting dick appointments with a sweet hillbilly who watches conservative news, but somehow still has a heart of gold. She said he isn't the best looking man, but he lets her spend the night at his house instead of parking on her street. Scout said they don't play old school video games, but he enjoys eating her cheesecake and banging her stunning body. She boastfully sent pictures of her bruised butt after she asked him to spank her, and when I said that looked too rough she just shrugged and said that's how she likes it. I felt unexpected jealousy. Scout suggested she felt relief knowing I still liked my gift so much, because if things continued going well with the sweet hillbilly she may not be available to take my virginity. I felt embarrassment that exceeded horny humiliation. She sensed I was unnerved, lamented that I didn't risk COVID when she wanted to spend the night, and suggested I take solace in not knowing what I was missing. While she taunted me I thumbed through bookmarks on my phone until I found the link to purchase my second book, and sent her all my published sex stories before hanging up.

The next day I shot awake to the intense commotion of Scout shouting and kicking at my front door. Aw hell she had my address after ordering the vagina sleeve. Scout raged at my door for a couple hours, but since I didn't have anywhere to be I let this attempted confrontation turn into a standoff of a couple hours more. I think in total Scout spent four hours yelling at my door. Well, she didn't yell the whole time. She took several breaks where I thought she had left, but I could peer through my blinds and see the top of her head which meant she was just sitting. For awhile she even broke out into song. She blew me up with texts and calls, but I never answered anything because, from the point of hanging up last night to now, this was still a ghosting. Her being on my porch didn't change that, but I was worried my reputation in my 1970's brick apartment complex was taking a hit. Finally she wandered off, but I needed another day before I felt comfortable going outside to empty trash or check the mail. Scout was never heard from again. Just kidding. She sent me random boob or butt photos for the next several months before giving up. When I noticed the longest stretch of not hearing from her, I looked her up on social media and she appeared to be in a happy relationship.

And that made me happy.

Okay so the story with Kasumi is nearly identical up until actually meeting. Kasumi was a hospital supervisor, and assured me that she had to take a daily COVID test. When I told Kasumi I was a virgin, she exclaimed, "Hell yeah! Come spend the night so I can take your virginity." After so many months of carefully participating in the partial lockdown, I figured I could go spend the night with a sexy hospital supervisor who had to test negative every 24 hours. Plus I hadn't been with an Asian woman before. So I went to Kasumi's huge house (hospital supervisor money), and she immediately told me to dress into my pajamas for bed. When I climbed into Kasumi's ridiculously tall bed, she straddled me and yelled, "Ready for me to take your virginity?" And she did. Enthusiastically. She was amazing. And I realized no woman now is ever going to provide the sustained virginity shaming I received as an awkward teenager because I had grown into myself too much. That good humiliation is no longer within reach. For a few more times, sex with Kasumi stayed very fun. I'd wake up at her house alone because of her important job, and shower with her hundreds of expensive shampoos and creams. But then something weird happened. Kasumi, despite being a hospital supervisor, started talking hillbilly nonsense about COVID being a fake, overblown threat that everybody is scared of for no reason. She even talked about dodging half her COVID tests because she didn't believe the virus could hurt her (apparently all those deaths had other explanations). Eventually, I lost the ability to get hard for her. So when I woke up one morning to Kasumi having left me my own house key, I responded with a treasure map to help her find where I buried it outside.

I went back into hiding for the rest of the summer.

Part 20

I go back to teaching

The good times couldn't last forever. Even though getting paid to stay home was absolutely amazing, and now I will always look toward that glorious future when something is done about the billionaires holding us hostage to slave wages, the COVID-19 summer finally faded away to the COVID Fall. The federally enhanced unemployment payments were still good for a few weeks into the school year, so I broke my heart canceling my remaining claim. I could get caught and in trouble if I continued drawing payments while teaching high school. There was also a lot of talk on the news about extending federally enhanced unemployment, but I figured whether payments were ripped away now or following a brief extension, there was no way for me to avoid going back to work forever. Funny how once upon a time I desperately wanted to become a full time charter school teacher, and now getting paid to stay home was the best job of my life (apologies to Esperanza Siempre).

After a whole summer of staying home, I was very shy venturing into the world again. Going to my charter school's corporate office was stressful. Going through the motions with HR regarding new employee on-boarding seemed senseless, and watching the sexual harassment videos with headphones in the middle of a busy office seemed superfluous. Couldn't the HR lady have sent me the forms electronically? Couldn't I have downloaded sexual harassment videos? My charter school company seemed to be operating as normal, but with employees wearing masks. And the wearing masks practice would diminish quickly no matter what was going on with community spread. So after my whole summer of living reclusively, and Arizona gaining no ground whatsoever in the fight against COVID, I was back in a professional setting like nothing happened. My eyes opened wide when the HR lady asked what my experience was like counseling juvenile probationers during the pandemic all summer. I forgot that four months ago I told her not to call Esperanza Siempre for a reference because I wasn't quitting until the school year. Wow, working that long would have been a huge waste of federally enhanced unemployment.

The charter school company, a for-profit organization, was called Cactus Academies. That corporate umbrella operated five charter high schools called Coyote Academy, Peccary Academy, Jackrabbit Academy, Tortoise Academy and Hummingbird Academy. I was hired to teach at Hummingbird Academy, but first I needed to report to Coyote Academy for new employee orientation. A mere week before school started, I assembled with everybody else hired by Cactus Academies for a thorough indoctrination. Coyote Academy was set up like its four sister schools, with a large central computer lab where students worked most of the day, flanked by a couple classrooms that teachers shared for small group instruction, and the principal's office and front desk services up front. I was immediately embarrassed to learn I committed to teaching in what was essentially a single room schoolhouse. For-profit education in Arizona just flings students who otherwise wouldn't graduate high school across the finish line. Hench the large computer lab where all the students keep clicking through five grueling hours a day. The small group classrooms were there so once every day we, the financially compensated adults, could pick a handful of students who were tired of clicking their mice and pretend we were teachers for about an hour each. The gist of our job was to maintain floor management and write bathroom passes.

New employee orientation at Coyote Academy was fucking weird. When we introduced ourselves, and answered the ice breaker questions (I hate two truths and a lie so much), we learned that Hummingbird Academy had three new English teachers starting at the same time. I spent all summer thinking I was an important content teacher only to learn I was one of several warm bodies sent to wander a warehouse of computers, a digital sweatshop, asking students if they needed help with any English related assignment or just another bathroom pass. If there were no specific students to help, I was to always scold everyone for loafing on their smartphones. We could not confiscate phones, but put phones in envelopes near the offenders. The other two English teachers were very young, fresh out of college, and ridiculously smart. While we sat in the computer lab, with every other seat marked unavailable by a "please social distance" sign taped to its corresponding monitor, I got to practice some of those mouse clicks my soon-to-be students would be making to advance toward their freebie high school diploma. I learned a student could graduate quickly by right-clicking every multiple choice question and using the browser's built in web search to instantly find every answer. By now, past students had already crowd sourced questions to the entire online curriculum used by Cactus Academies, and there were multiple websites boasting complete answer keys. The whole concept on display for me today encouraged cheating, and I was able to pass 20 percent of freshman English just dicking around for an hour at orientation. And even though my role humiliated me, I concluded this fake teaching bullshit was probably going to be my easiest job. If I could tough it out three years, I could cash out the sentence for a real teaching certificate.

The Cactus Academies' talking heads cheering on this big box version of education finally got around to sharing their plan for COVID. The school year was going to start with only teachers, but no students. For the first time in the history of the five schools, students were allowed to work from home. The curriculum had always been an online curriculum, but making students work in the supervised computer labs ensured they kept clicking five hours a day. Even though the diploma at the end is a freebie, students sure hated clicking five hours a day. Eventually, when community spread lowered to the first county determined benchmark, the Special Education students and English Second Language students would be allowed back in the building. Then, when community spread lowered to the next county determined benchmark, an initial wave of mainstream students would be allowed back in the building up to one-third capacity. After that there would be two more county determined benchmarks until we were allowed to fully open. As much as I wanted COVID to resolve for the good of mankind, I wasn't in a rush to see students fill up these schools. Sitting around offering remote assistance to students who were better off searching the Internet sounded like the next best thing to staying home. Just as I was finishing new employee orientation at Coyote Academy, and warming up to the idea of my easy job, I got a group text from some of the already established teachers inside Hummingbird Academy.

The first unknown coworker texted me, "Welcome to the Hummingbird Academy where we aren't afraid of COVID! Let's have a great year not living in fear!" I was not yet familiar with the Qanon cult, but a bunch of its looniest members worked at my new school.

2020

I BECOME A FAKE TEACHER

Part 21

(August) I start the school year

Administration
Principal Hillbilly

Curriculum Supervisor
Ms. Moon

Department of Math and Science
Ms. Catgastro
Mr. Dutch
Mr. Spudspank
Mr. Zenslack

Department of English and History
Ms. Guerrero
Mr. Kinkade (me)
Mr. Pecker
Mr. Pleats

     A weekend separated my orientation at a sister school from my first day reporting to the Hummingbird Academy, and part of me forgot how stupid a one room schoolhouse looked. When I walked in for the first time, I saw the familiar layout (from Coyote Academy) of a giant computer lab with every other seat marked off for social distancing. Hummingbird Academy was significantly larger, and, I later learned, the largest of the five charter high schools. There was already a smattering of teachers, but no students, and I guessed to take a seat anywhere I wanted to listen to the coming spiel from our principal. Eventually a loud, portly and unkempt woman with unappealing cleavage (similar to ribbed punching ball balloons with the rubber straps) lumbered in and introduced herself as Principal Hillbilly, immediately demanding we enter her digits into our phones ahead of any morning we may be running late. Yep, even with no students in the building, Principal Hillbilly set an expectation that she now controlled every minute of our schedules. Every afternoon thereafter warmed up to a swarm of adults simmering at the front door until the clock struck the exact minute we were allowed to exit the building. Principal Hillbilly squandered her first impression on other topics important to her, like her dumbass adult children, her two redneck divorces, her alleged boyfriend who is a principal at a district school, and the times she purportedly stopped school shootings by staying so intuitive and street smart. That first day was the most we ever saw Principal Hillbilly outside her office, because she also feared COVID-19 and had a sycophantic underling with the auspicious title of Curriculum Supervisor. Ms. Moon was Principal Hillbilly's right hand woman, who stood next to her throughout this opening morning monologue, nodding along and punching the air at every offbeat remark. Principal Hillbilly encouraged us to make lesson plans with the remaining time, and retreated to her office. Ms. Moon reiterated we were to make lesson plans with the remaining time, and retreated to her desk at the back of the computer lab. I realized the remaining time was literally seven hours and 45 minutes, and an online curriculum didn't require lesson plans. So I also guessed to take a seat anywhere, and surf the Internet until the exact minute I was allowed to exit the building.

We were all stuck in this drafty one room schoolhouse for the foreseeable future with nothing to do besides observe the assignments trickling in from students working from home. And the assignments trickling in were a drip not a stream. Since we were a credit recovery charter school on the south side of Tucson, most our students lacked consistent Internet access or needed to work longer hours at their essential service jobs to compensate for COVID's impact on their parents. Responding to the flow of online assignments probably took 20 minutes a day. Somehow our whole existence was predicated on appearing as a real school when all we did was write credit slips to students who passed online courses, and award freebie high school diplomas to students who the government wanted available for essential service jobs. Each online course had one "project" which was very loosely defined and required a teacher and student to briefly communicate on expectations. For English classes, that meant an essay from any topic covered in the course. These essays were the only piece of student work that required grading beyond pressing "OK" after a student finished all their clicks, and for awhile I took them seriously. However, students eventually called and complained because a precedent from years past had students trained that they could copy-and-paste their essays. Hummingbird students possessed literally no patience for even a single re-write. Principal Hillbilly dispatched Ms. Moon to tell me and the other newbie teachers to just apply a passing grade of 70 percent to any copied-and-pasted essay, and reasoned that knowing where to find information on the Internet was a legitimate academic skill. I told myself I only needed to be as ethical as the company cutting my checks, cracked my knuckles, and made muscle memory of the keystroke that confirmed 70 percent.

All of us sharing the 9 a.m. to 5 p.m. schedule was due to COVID's effect on the school year. Normally, our one room schoolhouse on the south side of Tucson would be open to three cascading sessions of students. Customers, which is how our internal documents referred to students, would choose to come in from 7 a.m. to noon, from noon to 5 p.m. or from 5 p.m. to 10 p.m. and all of us teachers would rotate through so at least one content teacher was available at all times. My normal schedule, with hours I worked later in the year, would have been 10 a.m. to 7 p.m. with a half hour lunch and a short planning day on Friday. Fridays were only available to students by request, and were otherwise for teachers. We teachers participated in a lot of fake planning. I came to understand the ubiquitous buzz about an initiative, or deliverable that always disappeared before its due date, as the pageantry of putting on a fake school for the benefit of business in Arizona. Somebody from under the tent of auditing could come in and ask, "What are you working on?" And we would always have an answer like, "Putting strategies into a binder to support Special Education and English Second Language Learning." In this environment, the faculty was slow to make friends. Or maybe we weren't used to expressionless masked faces, and needed more time to suss each other out. I came to know the teachers in my department before anybody else.

"This is kind of fucked up, right?" I asked Mr. Pecker, a handsome young English teacher with an unfortunately phallic sounding name that students loved to mock. "Indeed it is," he said, always speaking with an air of academics. Mr. Pecker knew I was commenting on our educator jobs being fake, and he provided some personal goal setting, "I love teaching, and this will get my foot in the door. I plan on writing real lessons that I will take with me when I eventually earn my professorship at a community college."

"I just love sports." Said Mr. Pleats, an equally handsome young History teacher who walked over to join our conversation now that the ice was broken by me acknowledging our educator jobs were entirely fake. He continued, "My girlfriend landed her dream job in Tucson, so I had to move with her and our dog from Florida. I had no idea I was qualified to teach history!" We all shared a laugh, but, while our educator jobs were fake as fuck, these two young just-out-of-college studs were the real deal. They had genuine hearts, empathy and intelligence in spades. Mr. Pecker passionately exposed our students to classic literature every chance he got, and Mr. Pleats, with his southern drawl, was always there to support anybody who needed help passing time throughout our boring marathon days by sustaining a conversation about sports, his dog, or his girlfriend's career. And Ms. Moon, while supervising the curriculum of every department, took a special interest in English, and spent most of her time with us (remember this for later). She was a 50 year old Native American woman who was still sexy. I liked her jet black hair, her firmly petite frame, and the way she barked orders all day. She quickly revealed herself as the author of that text I received goading COVID into giving us its best shot, because after we officially exchanged numbers she followed up with a lot of Republican propaganda against masks and social distancing. Finally, our department rounded out with Ms. Guerrero. She was a cantankerous old history teacher from a bygone era, fired from a district school after she dispensed corporal punishment against a disrespectful teenager. My colleagues thought she hated students, but a teacher doesn't show up on Valentine's Day with a headband of springy hearts, or on St. Patrick's Day with a headband of springy four-leaf clovers, because they hate students. No, to me, Ms. Guerrero just wanted school to look and feel like school.

That would never happen at the Hummingbird Academy.

Part 22

(September) I get to know the teachers

The days were long and painful. Only a handful of us at the Hummingbird Academy acted like COVID-19 was real, and made sure we wore masks and sanitized anything we touched after using it. Most of us were forgetful or ambivalent, and a small minority were vocally against the perceived democratic hoax or "plandemic." And even though the Qanon teachers were few in numbers, I remained disturbed that a place of learning had any Trump support at all. But the days were long and painful because we had no students and nothing to do. I efficiently shortened the time needed to award 70 percent to all the assignments in my grading queue down to ten minutes, and kept the better part of my eight hours for socializing with my colleagues and Qanon conspirators. Principal Hillbilly stayed in her office writing and rewriting the instructional schedule that would govern that mythical day we might have students in the building. Mr. Pecker spent his time reviewing the entire catalog of online English curriculum then packaging it into games his students could play over the Internet for "Pecker Points" he envisioned them trading in for prizes he would purchase before school opened in-person. Mr. Pleats continued chatting with all of us about sports, his dog, and his girlfriend's career, but, like Mr. Pecker, he drummed up the motivation to reach out to as many students working from home as he could, and also tried to make his History content immersive and interesting. I followed the example of the two younger male teachers, and also tried to engage my students. I wasn't as smart as Mr. Pecker, or as affable as Mr. Pleats, but, since I had a proclivity in popular culture and memes, I quickly built the most popular teacher website. I basically presented Mr. Pecker's total package, but through my own comedic medium, and his informative load resonated better as videos with me teaching them. More students interacting with my website translated to more completed assignments, and the workload drip finally swelled into a modest stream. For our effort, I was doling out many more 70's. Ms. Guerrero watched us from a distance, always grunting, snarling and judging. She had a gross habit of letting out an exasperated sigh every time she was upset, so we never stopped listening to her soundtrack of stern fatigue. Ms. Moon sauntered around supervising curriculum (whatever that means), and praised our department for its runaway success in lesson completion (lessons make up units, units make up courses, and courses make up credits).

Principal Hillbilly announced that while our student engagement was slightly above levels reported by our four sister schools, the corporate office was already worried that our projected number of graduates was going to be lower than expected. We were supposed to respond by putting on a drive-through graduation for last year's graduates, and then disseminate those images quickly to inspire current students working from home to spend more hours a day clicking. Principal Hillbilly reminded us that last year's graduates didn't get to walk after COVID hit, and assigned us all a section of names to call and hype this drive-through graduation experience. I wasn't cynical about a drive-through graduation if the students for whom it applied were interested, just awkward selling them caps and gowns when I had nothing to do with their accomplishment (since I wasn't there last year). Since most teachers were new this school year, conversations with last year's students went something like...

"Hi, this is Mr. Kinkade from the Hummingbird Academy-"

"Who the fuck is Mr. Kinkade?"

"Hi, this is Mr. Pecker from the Hummingbird Academy-"

"Hahahaha!"

"Hi, this is Mr. Pleats from the Hummingbird Academy-"

"Hi Mr. Pleats, what can I do for you?"

"Hi, this is Ms. Guerrero from the Hummingbird Academy-"

"You sound like a bitch."

"Hi, this is Ms. Moon from the Hummingbird Academy-"

"Hi Ms. Moon! I've missed you!"

Now that we had a project with some meaning outside our specific departments, I got to know the other teachers. Mr. Dutch was the first teacher outside of English and History to consistently seek me out for banter. He was an eccentric math teacher around my age who liked hard party drugs. He got off on mathematical theories, and spent nearly all his downtime creating computer models and running graphical simulations. He wasn't the only smart teacher around, in fact, roughly half of my colleagues were hella qualified and embarrassingly underused. I still don't understand the ruse of putting on a fake school while employing actual talent. But Mr. Dutch, like some of the other too-smart-for-this-school crowd, expressed his employment at Hummingbird Academy was a transitional move as he advanced his personal goal of getting back to the seaside location where he completed his past military obligations. He happened to drive the same make and model car as mine, but his entire driver's side was wrecked into oblivion. One day while leaving at the exact minute I was allowed to exit the building, I saw Mr. Dutch's car before I knew my car had a double, and experienced a conniption. Mr. Dutch was always up to mysterious shit on the weekend, and we all just assumed he led a double life as a government assassin or cartel sicario.

Ms. Catgastro was the other math teacher, and the only teacher in the entire faculty who had earned an official state teaching certificate that was achievable without having studied education in college, but only after putting in three years at a charter school. I wondered why if she was certified she hadn't moved on to a real school, but a lot of her strange behavior was representative of high functioning autism. She was very possessive of her seat, even when none of us had assigned seats. Remember, we were eight teachers occupying a giant computer lab meant to serve 300 credit recovery students who were now working from home, and could literally sit anywhere and still access the web interface we needed to confirm 70 percent on all the inbound assignments. Ms. Catgastro would begin and end every conversation with an update on her cat's life, and wanted to share every moment she captured in photo and video. I didn't mind humoring her, because there was nothing else to do, but I also found it amusing to amp my enthusiasm up to levels noticeable by nearby teachers, then send our fur baby mama to one of them with a well deployed, "Oh my God! You know who would love to see your cat topple off the laundry pile?? Mr. Dutch!! Go show Mr. Dutch right now!" And Ms. Catgastro would skip off toward Mr. Dutch who was left cursing me under his breath. The downside to Ms. Catgastro was her being another teacher in the Qanon cult. She would loudly watch aggressively patriotic videos about joining protests against masks, and lecture anybody she caught cleaning a keyboard or wiping down a monitor with an unwelcome ambush, "My dad from [backwoods hillbilly town] is very smart, and he found out that the plandemic is a democratic hoax to control all of us blah blah blah."

Critical thinking was stronger in the science department. Mr. Spudspank was another teacher around my age, but, like Mr. Dutch, he was also former military. Except he wasn't mysterious at all. In fact, he wore his heart on his sleeve, and was an earnest cheerleader for student and coworker success. Early into learning how to engage with students whose work was entirely online, I eavesdropped on quite a few phone calls Mr. Spudspank placed to students assigned to classes in his grading column. "Hey Brad, Chad, Brenda, Emily (whoever he was calling) this is Mr. Spudspank from your school checking in to make sure your username and password work, you know how to advance in the course, and you know how to highlight text and translate it into Spanish if needed." Of all of us at work, Mr. Spudspank spent the most time actually trying to spend the most time working. There wasn't too much he could do as a science teacher for students assigned to online classes who weren't even in the physical computer lab with us, but he kept calling them. Mr. Spudspank made his phone calls all day long, and seemed refreshed every time he connected with a student who hadn't previously answered. Unfortunately, students being teenagers, the kids who stood the most to benefit from a teacher checking in quickly blocked the school's phone number. This phenomenon became so challenging later in the year that the corporate decision making body flip flopped on allowing us to use texting apps in official communication. Texting students, while frowned upon in non-pandemic years, was a boon to actually getting them to respond. Mr. Spudspank was such a sweet man that his positive outlook frequently rubbed off on me, and I'd have spurts where I went all in on calling students and encouraging them to make those clicks toward their freebie high school diplomas.

The other half of the science department was an adorably chubby older gentleman named Mr. Zenslack who hobbled in late every day on a cane while wearing his fedora. Principal Hillbilly seemed wise enough to not go after a physically handicapped teacher's tardiness, but she absolutely watched the clock on everybody else. She watched the clock, but she was also stupid. Mr. Dutch and I only needed those first two months of school to figure out we could remove ourselves from the simmering swarm of humiliated teachers at the front door, and just dip out the back earlier and earlier. I'd like to brag about the size of my cojones, and while I took advantage of our idiot principal, Mr. Dutch was a legend in how much time he shaved off his school day. I might turn around after just two hours and discover he had given up just as soon as he tossed out his first batch of 70 percentages. But Mr. Zenslack was a different breed of renegade employee. Mr. Zenslack's first move after already coming in late was spending another 30 minutes preparing coffee and his breakfast platter. Then he would find the most unobservable seat to Ms. Moon's position in the room, and watch sports for the remainder of the day. Mr. Zenslack's claim to fame was that he never graded or wrote a credit slip the entire year. Mr. Pleats did all his grading for him, and was happy to do it. What I liked about our group was that most of us exalted those who were beating the system. In the dissent, Principal Hillbilly remained oblivious to Mr. Zenslack's lack of contribution toward giving students 70 percent on their assignments. Ms. Moon was loosely aware of how Mr. Zenslack spent his time, but didn't perceive him as fixable or harmful so left him alone. Ms. Guerrero may have taken up issue with Mr. Zenslack's laziness since he didn't fit her teaching worldview, but she also had some kind of gross crush on him and never grumbled like she would have if any of us so obviously took the same working vacation. So Ms. Catgastro was the only teacher to ever confront Mr. Zenslack with shit like, "Hey! What are you doing? Why are we all here?" To which he would passively respond, "Why are we here? Well, many religions have attempted to answer that…" And then he would outlast even her impressive patience for one-sided dialog with a colleague. I started bringing assorted pastries to the teachers' lounge most mornings simply because I enjoyed making Mr. Zenslack happy. We later learned that Mr.

Zenslack's home life was frequently in shambles whenever his 20-something stepson violated probation, which gave us all the more reason to cheer on his mantra of coming to work to relax.

The drive-through graduation wasn't the blowout event corporate envisioned, but the eight of us waved banners congratulating last year's students who rolled through in a small caravan of cars. A highlight included a drunk mom flashing us, and screaming, "My baby graduated!"

Part 23

(October) I fear the teachers

I can't report enough just how strange I felt going from a summer of caution to a Fall of flamboyancy. Like, the Hummingbird Academy had all this corporate signage about COVID-19, no students working in-person, and a flimsy cleaning schedule we supposedly shared, but by October the eight of us were sitting closely together, and used holding coffee cups or candy bars as legitimate reasons to hang the face mask off to one side. The flimsy cleaning schedule was another area where Mr. Pecker shined. Still with those mythical plans that on any given day students might be back in the building, corporate sent us a leaf blower like contraption rigged up to a tank of disinfectant. While held at the correct angle, the "fogger" as we called it would produce a purifying cloud of disinfectant which ideally could sanitize the 300 computers very quickly. Principal Hillbilly scheduled all of us to take turns "fogging" the school as practice for when we needed to preform the feat quickly between the three sessions of school. But more often than not we just let Mr. Pecker fog, and as long as Principal Hillbilly heard the mechanical grinding noise she never asked questions. If Ms. Moon attempted to fog she failed at aiming the machine at the correct angle, and shot pure fluid directly into the computers, ruining several of them. Principal Hillbilly complained about the number of computers going down, but never resolved the root cause. Good guy Mr. Pecker did his best to beat Ms. Moon to the fogger at cleaning time, but Ms. Moon enjoyed pretending to work. Or worse, maybe she thought she was working.

As leader of the Hummingbird Academy's Qanon faction, Ms. Moon derived great joy any time she could get those of us taking COVID seriously to participate in a superspreader event. Early in the year, Ms. Moon laid out plans to continue monthly teacher team building events as they happened in years past. To my credit, when the first group email arrived from her dictating, "Building a strong team dynamic for the day students fill up this school is more important than fearing COVID. Please vote by reply-all if you'd rather we get together at the cinema for a movie and popcorn, a restaurant for drinks and trivia, or a bowling alley for pins and billiards," I was the first to reply with, "I am not comfortable participating in anything for which I am not contractually obligated, but the rest of you have fun." And then thankfully reasonable voices like Mr. Dutch, Mr. Spudspank, and Mr. Zenslack chimed in with agreement. "Not a good idea," Replied Mr. Dutch. "Best to wait," said Mr. Spudspank. "If we all go down, there won't be any teachers available to help students," added Mr. Zenslack. The younger guys, Mr. Pecker and Mr. Pleats, didn't feel like making waves, but felt represented by us older guys who spoke out against the onslaught of stupid superspreader suggestions. While Ms. Catgastro and Ms. Guerrero were squarely with Qanon, they weren't in a rush to party with Ms. Moon and kept quiet in these particular debates. Ms. Moon was left with no support, and just raged back in emails, "You all are letting fear control you! Just like the government wanted." Then the next week she would be back with, "How about a potluck where we all just bring delicious dishes from home?" Still no.

Unfortunately, while there were superfluous superspreader events I could kill with the support of like minded coworkers, there were equally superfluous superspreader events I couldn't kill because they happened inside the school by order of the principal. Principal Hillbilly announced the traditional Halloween door decorating contest, and paired us off into groups of three-ish. There was Mr. Pecker, Mr. Pleats, and Ms. Guerrero at the door to the teachers' lounge. There was Mr. Dutch, Mr. Spudspank, and Mr. Zenslack at the door to the small group classroom (remember that's the side space we could siphon off students for more traditional learning if they were in the main computer lab for in-person school). And there was me, Principal Hillbilly, Ms. Moon and Ms. Catgastro at the door to Principal Hillbilly's office. "Why the hell are we doing this?" I thought to myself on the day everybody arrived with artsy things to gussy up the doors. At first, I tried to hide, but Principal Hillbilly shouted, "Mr. Kinkade! Get over here!" Forcing me to crowd around the door to her office, passing paper pumpkins and frilly ghosts to her and Ms. Moon as they asked for them. When all was said and done, Mr. Dutch, Mr. Spudspank, and Mr. Zenslack created a terrifying door that looked like a portal to hell, complete with a prism laser light show and rising fog. Mr. Pecker, Mr. Pleats, and Ms. Guerrero created a literary amalgamation of famous monster novels like Frankenstein and Dracula, with tons of associated iconography. And finally, Principal Hillbilly and Ms. Moon created the most basic Halloween scene with the most obvious clip-art from the well of school supplies already owned by the academy. Throughout the decorating, Ms. Catgastro would continually apply wallet-sized sticker photos she printed of her cat in its Halloween costume before Ms. Moon peeled them off. Now Hummingbird Academy had three Halloween doors that would still be there after Christmas.

Then Ms. Moon finally won her first off-campus event. I was blindsided when in response to Ms. Moon's next attempt at corralling us in the community, Principal Hillbilly chimed in with a, "Let's do it! I've been getting bored in this building, and we had so much fun decorating doors." Principal Hillbilly and Ms. Moon assembled us at a park in Principal Hillbilly's neighborhood, and I took ridiculous photographs of teachers packed tightly together at picnic tables under ramadas with posted signs saying the park amenities and equipment were closed for COVID. Like, that's a true story. I still have team bonding pictures of us behind warning signs and blockades. The games Principal Hillbilly and Ms. Moon planned involved as much COVID cross-contamination as possible. I, kid you not, Principal Hillbilly instructed us to remove our masks, look up, and fold our arms behind our backs while Ms. Moon walked by and placed cookies on our faces. The game's objective was to jostle and squirm around to get the cookies to travel into our mouths instead of falling onto the ground. Now that Principal Hillbilly was having as much fun as Ms. Moon, the superspreader events gained traction and took off in a big way. The movies, restaurants and sports I successfully shot down those early months were fair game, and my anxiety that my coworkers were trying to kill me was dialed up to ten. Even teachers previously on my side left the trenches and proposed superspreader events they thought were "OK" because they were more personal and smaller in scale. Such as Mr. Spudspank's housewarming party or Mr. Pecker's fantasy card game night. I was glad so many of us were friends, but felt like teachers needed to set a better example for students and families. The health department still wanted people to social distance, and COVID was still killing.

Part 24

(November) I can't fix education

Since charter schools hire a lot of fake teachers (like me) part of the pageantry includes meetings called "professional development" that are supposed to be the principal or other experts bringing staff with non-education related degrees up to speed on learning standards and basics. Our schedules included daily professional development, but since Principal Hillbilly lived in her office, we met with her over video conferencing software. We would either log in from any random seat or, a small group of us, maybe me and the two other old guys, would sit together in the side classroom and log in over the big screen. Professional Development at Hummingbird Academy was just Principal Hillbilly waxing poetic about her favorite topics, such as her dumbass adult children, her two redneck divorces, her alleged boyfriend who is a principal at a district school, and the times she purportedly stopped school shootings by staying so intuitive and street smart. One time we logged in for professional development, or PD as the meeting was also called, and sat through Principal Hillbilly wrapping up nauseating sex talk with that district school principal boyfriend for whom she was so proud. The day after he dumped her, she drew her office blinds shut and cried for two weeks. So while the idea behind professional development made sense, helping non-teachers grow into teachers, there was never anything to talk about when all the students needed to do to graduate was keep making mouse clicks. The truly interesting PDs happened when Ms. Moon ran them. She at least tried to pick an educational topic, but then distracted herself with Qanon theories. The video conferencing suite that hosted our PDs included message boards, which Ms. Moon filled up with Qanon shit posts. Since there didn't seem to be a principal or corporate level consequence for posting unprofessionally, I started talking back to Ms. Moon and outright trolling her fringe right-wing beliefs. And while Ms. Moon never backed away from her wild conspiracy theories even in the face of overwhelming evidence, she also never rage quit our conversations. She and I began fighting and then flirting in perpetuity.

My professional development really paid off when we finally received our first three students in the building. Just kidding, my PD never paid off. But we did receive our first three students in the building when one of the probation officers in the zip code stopped by and asked if we could take some juvenile probationers who weren't staying home and preventing community spread, but rather gang banging while their parents were at work. I said what's up to the probation officer since she and I worked closely together while I was with Esperanza Siempre, and she responded that she had wondered where I went and where I was hiding out. I shrugged and let her know I got fired for quitting. Of the three students she wanted us to keep an eye on, one of them was actually a former counseling client of mine. I wasn't thrilled to have students in the building as a court condition of release because the arrangement made babysitters out of teachers, and we understood these particular young people were running around town doing sketchy shit without regard to pandemic precautions. When Santiago, Diego and Fernando showed up, I pulled Santiago aside and asked him why he was still on probation so long after I counseled him at Esperanza Siempre. Santiago struggled with the transition from calling me by my first name to calling me the Mr. nonsense required at the school. Santiago told me he was now on ankle monitor and a single violation away from going to county jail. I rarely saw young people screw up so badly that juvenile detention was no longer an option, but that outcome did happen. Santiago also told me his family's horses had been winning lots of races because he gives them cocaine. Santiago enjoyed showing me the fat rolls of cash he always had on him, and all I could do was encourage him to keep his mask on and get back to clicking on schoolwork. Diego also struggled to keep his mask on, but was otherwise a polite teenager with a goofy smile (a smile I should have never seen if he could wear his damn mask longer than five minutes). I once caught Diego hitting his vape on the side of the gas station facing the school, and approached him to suggest smoking on the side not visible to the faculty. The fucker ran from me, so when I saw him in the computer lab an hour later I let him know I just wanted him aware that Principal Hillbilly can see the shaded side of the gas station from her window. I said I don't care what he does off the property, he knows smoking is bad for his health, just be smart about it. Then I relentlessly teased him for running from me. Fernando, the soft spoken bigger dude, seemed to space out the five hours a day he was punished to sit in our computer lab, but once agreed to follow me into the side classroom. I walked him through the junior class essay which was a comparison of Lincoln's 'House Divided' speech, Whitman's 'O Captain!' poem, and the Illinois 'Hull House' charter. I enjoyed this essay assignment because if done correctly students would see how Lincoln put forth an important idea, his idea became meaningful and romanticized, and then finally his idea became a foundational force for good. When we finished, Fernando took a photo of his essay and texted it to his mom. He told me his mom would be proud he wrote his first five paragraph essay. I congratulated him, awarded more than 70 points, and then sent him back into the computer lab to keep clicking.

Three students in the building broke Principal Hillbilly's brain because all year thus far she wrote and rewrote the instructional schedule preparing for this moment. Now she handed out these convoluted micro-schedules we were to follow throughout our day that included times we were allowed to be sitting down engaging with our students working from home, and times we were supposed to be on our feet "proctoring" which meant providing floor management and assisting students in the building. Except she scheduled the bulk of everyone's time as proctoring, which meant six out of the eight of us were always up watching only three students. Sometimes one of us would ignore the instructional schedule and sit down to catch up on our grading queue, which would without fail trigger Principal Hillbilly into sending a group email about how the instructional schedule is to be faithfully followed at all times. I started having nightmares that somehow my mom or dad would find out my job as an unexceptional late thirties male was to spend the majority of my day at work walking around an empty computer lab. If any of the six given teachers banned from sitting at a computer that hour included Ms. Catgastro or Ms. Guerrero they would hog the three boys whose consequence was school, and make sure the unlucky probationers only worked on their specific curriculum. If my zigzagging around the computer lab happened to zag me near Santiago, Diego or Fernando then Ms. Guerrero would scream, "Don't disturb them! They're working on my class right now!" And the sad boys would glance toward me with a look of defeat, wishing Ms. Guerrero would reach the sit down portion of her instructional schedule so they could return to looking up answers on the Internet unsupervised.

I didn't take a victory lap when Trump lost the November election, but my relief was palpable. To the contrary, Ms. Catgastro became more vocal in trying to rally support for a teacher mask protest (failed). Ms. Guerrero started wearing "All Lives Matter" shirts (stupid). And Ms. Moon switched up what she had been saying all year, and told me how proud she was that a woman of color "like her" was going to be sworn in as Vice President (hot). Ms. Moon also told me I was too good looking to carry the gear I brought to school each day in a reusable grocery bag, and to please send her a link to the briefcase or "man bag" I wanted online so she could purchase me an upgrade. When I didn't take her request seriously, she went about purchasing me $500 in gifts on her own. I knew Ms. Moon had a man at home she referred to as her "partner," but assumed if she were openly buying me extravagant gifts then she and her partner must have some polyamorous arrangement. Without the prospect of four more years of Trump, I needed a new distraction so I started flirting more with Ms. Moon. I signed onto our video conferencing suite and down-voted all her latest posts about how democrats stole the election. I had already figuratively walked Santiago, Diego and Fernando through their English class essays, so there was nothing else to do except literally walk around the building during the proctoring hours of my instructional schedule. The students working from home still sent in garbage essays that they copied-and-pasted from online encyclopedias. And sometimes the copy-and-paste job was so haphazard that the essay included remnants of the footnoted HTML. Boom! 70 percent.

Part 25

(December) I make out at the Christmas party

Do dreams come true? I once stood inside Arizona's Department of Education Career Fair, wishing a charter school would give me a chance to switch from social work to teaching, as part of my bigger dream of earning my state teaching certification. Now there I was teaching hybrid instruction to students in a South side credit recovery high school during America's first year of COVID-19. That former, older male coworker who encouraged me to write my second book (the raunchy sex book) used to say, "There's nothing worse than a man who gets exactly what he wants then complains about it." In his context he meant himself after he applied for a supervisor position and immediately regretted it. Middle management is usually terrible, and that's coming from me as a former group home supervisor (who eschewed climbing the ladder any higher). Most middle managers think that if they're just terrible enough to their workers then the corporate big shots will take notice and invite them into the exclusive club. But most middle managers are infinitesimally closer to the workers they detest than any corporate elite they idealize. One reason Principal Hillbilly was so adamant we "always be walking" was because corporate visitors scolded principals for teachers sitting at computers. Even though with COVID the majority of our students were on their computers at home, and likewise needed teachers at computers on the other end, Principal Hillbilly still wanted to visually pan the floor and observe teachers scurrying around the empty lab like little lost souls. Ms. Moon wasn't even a middle manager, but convinced herself she was on a fast track to club corporate. Our flirting got so dirty that we moved it off the faculty message board and spent the day texting each other.

The invitation to December's bombastic superspreader event came in the form of a White Elephant Gift Exchange. This particular party asked that everybody bring a wrapped present under 20 dollars in value, and Principal Hillbilly's email made very clear that alcohol was not only allowed, but encouraged. Our three students wouldn't be in the building the final day of this quarter because that Friday was marked for teacher grading. Teacher grading at the Hummingbird Academy was so funny because students always got 70 percent no matter what, but the only variable was how many clicks they had made toward that 70 percent. So there was a tedious process where we had to go through our whole roster of students one by one and sort them into two categories, "Making adequate progress" or "Not making adequate progress." And that's the only report card information parents ever received from us. Even though I had participated in several superspreader events up to Christmas, the early news of COVID vaccines imbued me with new determination not to catch the virus before the chance to be inoculated. So I knew I wanted to call out sick for the gift exchange, problem being that the schedule for Friday was to complete student grading up until lunchtime, and then hold the gift exchange from lunchtime to the end of the day. I decided the best course of action was to secretly finish my grading on Thursday, and then call out sick Friday morning. Although I picked a seat in the farthest corner of the computer lab, plenty of teachers strolled over to me during their proctoring time and asked, "Are you grading already?" And I just let them think I needed a head start because the process was still unnatural to me, a mere social worker posing as a teacher. When I called out sick to Principal Hillbilly the next day, and assured her I already finished my grading, she just thanked me for being on top of things and wanted to know if I had also left a wrapped bottle of alcohol.

I relaxed for a few minutes before Ms. Moon blew up my phone, demanding to know why I called out sick when I wasn't sick. At this point, the faculty just assumed my absence during superspreader events was pure not wanting to participate in more superspreader events. I told Ms. Moon very bluntly that I was going to avoid her and everybody else until I completed my vaccine series. The health department was already inventing a Priority List, and teachers were going to be in Priority 1B. Our priority pissed me off because I knew Businesswoman from Esperanza Siempre was going to be in Priority 1A, and get vaccinated before me despite all her early efforts to help COVID spread as far and wide as possible. Esperanza Siempre as a "healthcare clinic" was ahead of Hummingbird Academy as a school. I frequently had to combat my vaccine envy with positive self talk about how the most reckless people getting vaccinated first was still a net gain to the world. Ms. Moon got some digs in about me living my life in fear, but then begged me to let her come deliver more holiday gifts to my apartment after the Christmas party. She swore up and down she would wear her mask so I relented. Two things about Ms. Moon raised my kink flag, she was an older woman and she was in a position of authority over me. Waiting for her to come over tore me in half because while I was about to be hosting a sexy 50 year old Native American woman, said 50 year old Native American woman was also a Qanon COVID superspreader nut job that would probably get me killed.

True to her word, Ms. Moon arrived at my door wearing a mask. She brought me several nice gifts, plenty of which were luxury liquors. She asked if I had shot glasses, and off came the mask. I only had shot glasses from various trips, either mine or those of past coworkers. I set out a shot glass from my trip to Chicago for counseling certification and a shot glass from the free swag at the Department of Education Career Fair. Ms. Moon and I toasted the start of Christmas vacation, which was a new perk to me. A benefit to working at a charter school (or any school) was having the same time off as the students, minus a day or two for finishing grading and last minute administration. Ms. Moon began pouring additional shots, and seductively putting my glass up to my lips for me then pouring the alcohol into my mouth. "Ah the hell with it," I thought. Our school's biggest Qanon COVID superspreader was already unmasked in my apartment, "If she has COVID then I already do, too." I grabbed Ms. Moon's waist and pulled her into me. We aggressively and drunkenly made out for several hot minutes then Ms. Moon started pulling her clothes up and to the sides to show me random spiritual or tribal tattoos that had remained hidden until now. I complimented these disclosures and sensually kissed her on some of her tattoos before resuming to make out. We kissed a lot more, and my erection was ready to tear through my pants. Ms. Moon spun around, whipping me with her waist length black hair, and said she needed to use my bathroom. I sat on the couch, and yelled for her to hurry up because my dick was harder than it had been all year. She emerged, and said, "That's great, but don't show it to me yet!" Ms. Moon said she was not in a polyamorous relationship, and that she hadn't kissed another man in ten years.

She said she wanted to see how she felt for awhile, and would send me some hot pictures later while she thought it over. Her confirmed relationship status made me nervous because I immediately knew her boyfriend was a giant Trump supporter. How could he not be? There was no other way a 50 year old Native American woman would have found the Qanon cult on her own. Ms. Moon kissed me goodbye and went home.

My Christmas break didn't get far before Ms. Moon's texts suddenly didn't sound like her. "Who the fuck is this? If you text this number again I will kill you, and that's a fucking promise!" I closed my eyes in a moment of reflection, wondering why I allowed this to happen. I had known for so long not to get involved with coworkers. I convinced myself that the COVID situation made drama more appealing than normal. We had so little to do all day, any little thread of drama was worth pulling on for the mental (and then physical) stimulation. But now I had a right-wing firearms enthusiast blowing up my phone, possibly with my address if Ms. Moon had saved my street inside my contact information. I only sent a single text back, and vaguely commented, "I don't know who this is, but I report death threats to the police." I really hoped Ms. Moon's boyfriend didn't have access to our entire texting history, and assumed my chance of surviving the night was fifty-fifty. About two hours later, Ms. Moon called and said that while she was in the shower, her boyfriend looked at her phone and saw some flirtatious comments, but lucky for us, nothing too incriminating. Ms. Moon said her strategy all along had been read, respond, and delete (whew). She said her boyfriend threw her phone behind the couch, and took off for a drunken drive. She added that she didn't think he was headed my way, but don't open my door tonight. I asked her to delete my information from her phone, and she agreed. When Ms. Moon called me again the next day to report me being in the clear, she proposed we continue our pseudo sexy relationship, but disengage every day before the boyfriend comes home at 5 p.m. I said that no, we needed to be done permanently for my peace of my mind. Ms. Moon said that would depress her, but she understood. When school resumed, Ms. Moon and I never spoke again. If she had school business, she relayed the information through Mr. Pecker or Mr. Pleats. Everybody intuitively knew Ms. Moon and I were on the other side of a Christmas falling out.

I COMMIT HIGH SCHOOL CREDIT FRAUD IN ARIZONA

Part 26

(January) I become the yearbook teacher

The New Year brought a quarter of the students back in the building, not because COVID-19 was under control, but because the Arizona governor crippled our local leaders' ability to properly mitigate the pandemic. The governor sabotaged mayors and city councils back when he thought he had a chance in Trump's second term cabinet, and continued to minimize COVID when he thought he could ride a MAGA wave into the Senate some day. More students in the building meant more waiting-on-vaccine stress for me. We opened the doors to students classified as Special Education or English Second Language and still we mostly got the discipline challenges. Not only did probation dump a fresh handful of juvenile offenders on us, but parents fed up with their teenagers having unapproved friends over and just generally loafing around or having sex all day also added to the in-person attendance pile. Principal Hillbilly put us on the regular schedule where a third, a third, and a third of us worked different, but overlapping shifts. The good news was that Ms. Moon was in the first wave, and I was in the second wave, so I didn't have to see her a full shift. Although teenagers lacked the ability to keep a face mask on properly, some of them were cool and respectful enough to add worthwhile conversations into my day. None of them particularly enjoyed the online curriculum, or making all those clicks they needed to make for five hours every day, but they didn't hold it against us. They all had a story to share about how their efforts fell apart in regular high schools, and why they were now looking to get that freebie high school diploma as soon as possible.

I built up warm rapports with a lot of the students because of my counseling background and natural empathy, but if they needed true academic help in English I usually brought Mr. Pecker over to see them. Sometimes I would feel guilty for the couple of students who hadn't yet discovered that all the answers to the entire online high school curriculum, leased by the corporate business office and disseminated through the five schools, were conveniently online, and struggled with the ethics of just cluing them into the scam. If nine students were cheating and flying through their classes, was I fair to allow one student to plod along attempting the material and questions? Another conundrum was that a significant swath of the students had forgotten how to be students, and could easily spend their entire five hour session on their smartphones. I tried to explain to them that running out the clock was only an accomplishment in a regular school, and if a student didn't finish a credit recovery course by the end of the school year in our charter format then they had to start over next year. There was a rule of thumb that encouraged finishing seven to twelve percent of a class per week if working on all five classes, or increase the weekly percent per class worked on in lieu of the ignored class (like if a student wanted to knock out all of math before moving onto science). Of course none of the students followed our advice, and just looked up answers on the Internet until they ran out of steam for the day. Other ways they forgot how to be students included getting up without permission, and claiming they were "starving" upon arrival. All of which was annoying only because Principal Hillbilly sent us harassing emails every time she saw a student eating at a computer or coming back from the restroom without a pass. My job devolved into redirecting students from their smartphones and writing them bathroom passes, exactly as explained to me in new hire orientation.

Although Ms. Guerrero and Ms. Catgastro were fiercely possessive of their specific classes and the students currently clicking on them, Principal Hillbilly relentlessly told us that any and all students were always all of our students. So if a student asked me a math question, and Mr. Dutch or Ms. Catgastro were not available, then I would still have to attempt to help. Students so rarely had academic questions because teachers weren't needed when all the answers were available online, that when genuine student interest did ignite a stimulating discussion the interaction attracted several of us.

If a student asked me about Animal Farm because the book was in their English course, Mr. Pleats might come over with supplemental information about the Russian revolution, followed by Mr. Spudspank showing up to talk about the science and technology behind farming. In one such event, our recently added student, Maria, was asking me and Mr. Spudspank how to approach the project due in Ms. Guerrero's class. I immediately offered to fetch Ms. Guerrero, but Maria begged me not to because, in her words, "Ms. Guerrero's a bitch, and talking to her triggers me." Maria's project asked that she write a few paragraphs on how two government agencies might work together in response to a natural disaster. Maria struggled with the internal motivation needed to fill up the blank page with sentences until Mr. Spudspank offered the brilliant idea to write about a hypothetical zombie apocalypse. "I can do that?" Asked Maria. "Why not?" Answered Mr. Spudspank, further explaining, "The heart of this assignment is understanding the relationship between government agencies, so I recommend using the trope of a zombie apocalypse as a jumping off point for how FEMA, the military, Health and Human Services, Border Control, and Homeland Security might rally and respond." I nodded in admiration as Mr. Spudspank lit the spark of learning in Maria, and we walked off as she started researching and writing. The next day, as soon as Maria's finished assignment hit Ms. Guerrero's grading queue, the ornery old History teacher let out a massive, "What the fuck is this shit?!"

Ms. Guerrero went into full spectacular meltdown. She demanded to know why Maria thought she could write about a "Zombie Apocalypse" in a serious school assignment. Maria, not wanting to implicate me or Mr. Spudspank, held her own for a few minutes while repeatedly warning Ms. Guerrero to get the fuck out of her face. The profanity triggered Ms. Guerrero even more, who then hollered and hollered for Principal Hillbilly. Mr. Spudspank was quicker than me, but the two of us bolted over to Maria and Ms. Guerrero. "I gave her the idea! I'm sorry!" Mr. Spudspank frantically explained, "This is not her fault. I thought we had a creative way to make the assignment interesting." I arrived for additional support, and threw in my two cents with much more amusement than Mr. Spudspank, "Ms. Guerrero, if COVID mutates enough then we may need Maria's work as a blueprint for how to actually respond in a zombie apocalypse." Maria and I snickered while Ms. Guerrero went nuclear about how nobody at the Hummingbird Academy, not student, not teacher, not administrator, took education seriously. Except Ms. Guerrero forgot that corporate considered students customers, and Principal Hillbilly dove into the scene and fired Ms. Guerrero on the spot. As Principal Hillbilly escorted Ms. Guerrero out of the building, Ms. Guerrero still ranting about all of us spending the year in opposition to her, Mr. Spudspank lost the color in his face.

"I can't believe I cost Ms. Guerrero her job." The science teacher struggled to come to terms.

"Nah, fuck that bitch." Maria declared. I had to agree that Ms. Guerrero picked a low hill to die on. Barely a mound, really. Most students submitted copied-and-pasted crap for their projects, but Maria actually spent a day working on a writing assignment. "Mr. Spudspank," I assured him, "You are a great educator and an inspiring figure." Principal Hillbilly came back from firing Ms. Guerrero, and yelled, "Mr. Kinkade, you're the new yearbook teacher!" Then she returned to her office and slammed her door, briefly reopening it to add, "And I don't think Ms. Guerrero even recruited yearbook students so you better fucking hurry."

"What the fuck?" I asked aloud.

"Sucks to suck!" Giggled Maria.

"Funny, Maria! Welcome to Yearbook Club." I jeered back.

"Aw fuck!"

Part 27

(February) I get vaccinated

Teaching yearbook turned out better than expected. Yearbook production always attracted a special kind of student who possessed chutzpah. Not only did I bond with students on a level more personal than awarding 70 percent at the end of their clicks, but we entered a symbiotic relationship that made everybody's day better. Students didn't like to sit at a computer for five straight hours as much as I didn't like to stand in an enduringly empty computer lab the better part of eight hours. If I wrote my students a "yearbook pass" then they could freely walk around the room, and if I said I was constructing the actual yearbook pages then I could freely sit on my ass in the same room. Bye, bye instructional schedule! Maria and I recruited other students, Sofia and Luz, to help us publish a yearbook in half the time as the other schools since Ms. Guerrero had signed up for this responsibility and then never thought about it again. For their efforts, Maria, Sofia and Luz got to replace an English course, and I got a $500 stipend for teaching an additional class. Obviously we repurposed the zombie apocalypse essay for the first article, and then came up with filler ideas since a one room schoolhouse lacked opportunities to take interesting photos or report on interesting events. The challenge was compounded by most of the students working from home. We photographed students in the building, and solicited selfies from those working outside of the building. We also asked, via my teacher website, for photos of home computer setups and animal companions. The girls also posted surveys and requested artwork. The pages filled up quickly. Maria had a small baby at home, and was studying to be a nurse. Or at least she would be studying to be a nurse after we awarded her the freebie high school diploma. Sofia was shy and wanted to make friends through the yearbook since sitting at a computer all day didn't afford the same chance to form friendships as a regular school. Luz was going through a mental health crisis since a recent family move to Tucson separated her from her longtime girlfriend, and she caught that girlfriend posting photos on social media with another girl. Luz thought joining yearbook could be a distraction or at least afford her more time to talk through her troubles with me and the girls. Whenever Luz got depressed over her ex-girlfriend, Maria rallied her to "forget that cheating bitch!" And Sofia built her up with the affirmation, "You are a Queen! You will find somebody better." Maria, Sofia, and Luz became fast friends, and creating that opportunity for them was probably my greatest COVID-19 year accomplishment. The yearbook certainly didn't sell.

Yearbook kept me comfortably distracted until suddenly HR sent an email that contained our vaccination letters. I opened the attached PDF, and read the first few words, "To whom it may concern, Jason Kinkade is a teacher providing in-person instruction at the Hummingbird Academy, a charter school of Cactus Academies..." and then thought, "Holy fucking shit! This is it!" I felt dizzy. Priority 1B was here, and I could finally get my first dose of that sweet COVID vaccine. I closed my eyes and imagined how relieved I would feel coming to work with all the students who wore their masks below their nose, and all my Qanon colleagues who thought the virus was a democratic hoax. I pretended I needed to work on the yearbook, but sat and struggled to confirm my appointment. For some reason, the calendar confirmation part of the Health Department's website kept saying Priority 1B hadn't started despite the introduction page saying otherwise. I ended up registering as Priority 1A instead and selected substance abuse counselor as my job. I was going to flip my shit if nobody checked my vaccination letter, and I could have claimed a social work identity all along. Now that I had an appointment that was still two weeks away, my perception of time slowed to a crawl. Students talking to me with masks below noses, colleagues hacking and coughing, the Qanon cult touching doorknobs, and the fogger sputtering and ruining computers all moved at one tenth regular speed, and I convinced myself COVID was going to hit me before my appointment.

Corporate approved getting vaccines during the school day so long as there were still other teachers in the building, but regardless I searched for the first available spot and found availability very early in the morning. I happily woke up before sunrise, downed my coffee, and was first in line at the hospital that turned its parking garage into a drive-through vaccination clinic. This was also the same hospital where Kasumi worked, and I wondered if she ever changed her mind on COVID being a democratic hoax. I also wondered (hypothetically) if my dick would get hard for her again after I was vaccinated, but mostly because I was beginning to worry about whether I'd be impotent in my forties. I hurriedly voided my bladder full of coffee into my emergency pee bottle I kept under my seat before security waved me, and the line of cars behind me, into the first checkpoint. One checkpoint ensured I had an appointment, and the second checkpoint verified my insurance (even though uninsured could also get shots), and guess what? Nobody asked to see my vaccination letter confirming I was a high school teacher. I was so disappointed I didn't try to come as Priority 1A! Finally, I reached the stop where a clinician administered the COVID vaccine, provided me the little vaccine passport and a second appointment, and directed me to an aftercare parking space where I would need to idle ten minutes in case my body reacted. I felt so goddamn relived. Even though I knew I needed that second dose for maximum immunity, I felt better than I had felt since I was with Esperanza Siempre at the start of the pandemic. I went back to Hummingbird Academy walking on sunshine. Qanon teacher Ms. Catgastro was just going about her day, completely indifferent to her Priority 1B status, and Qanon Curriculum Supervisor Ms. Moon had already scheduled her vaccine appointment. Somehow Ms. Moon's political rhetoric died down when she realized she could get something other people really wanted way before they could. The typical symptoms associated with the COVID vaccine hit me that night, and I felt nauseous and shivered under my blankets with a big smile on my face.

Most of Hummingbird Academy got the vaccine. Principal Hillbilly took time out of the day to get her vaccine, and we enjoyed a nice afternoon session where she wasn't bitching about the instructional schedule. Ms. Moon got her vaccine because she was a hypocrite, and only truly believed in Qanon because of her psycho boyfriend. Mr. Spudspank, Mr. Pecker and Mr. Pleats all got their vaccines reasonably soon. Mr. Dutch may or may not have gotten his vaccine. He kept telling us he scheduled appointments, but then didn't wake up promptly on the other side of his drug and alcohol binges. There was a period where none of the vaccination sites would reschedule Mr. Dutch because he missed too many attempts. Mr. Zenslack was lazy and put his vaccine off until after he almost died from COVID, but then he finally got it. Principal Hillbilly and

Ms. Moon scheduled a post-vaccination party at a bar after everybody's first dose, and I rolled my eyes at how stupid our leadership was to throw yet another superspreader shindig before anybody on staff received the second shot. Two weeks later, following another early as possible appointment, I came to school fully vaccinated. I walked right up to Mr. Spudspank full of joy and enthusiasm, and vigorously victory-humped his computer monitor while he was typing. "Uhhh…" He said, nodding toward my yearbook girls who were giggling and snapping pictures of me being lewd.

"Don't put that in the yearbook!" I yelled.

Principal Hillbilly completely ruined the yearbook. Maria, Sofia, and Luz all cried the day Principal Hillbilly berated me for "letting the students do whatever they wanted without supervision or direction" and sent me back to tell them that all their original artwork was going to be replaced with the most obvious clip-art from the well of school supplies already owned by the academy. Principal Hillbilly's complaints included that too much art was about hummingbirds (well that's the name of the stupid school), all the words that were included in artwork were drawn in a "gang style that looked like spray-paint" (so what, calligraphy), and that our entire tome made the school look "ghetto" (oh my God, she thought the school held a prestigious reputation). Principal Hillbilly called me back a second time to keep ranting after she got the impression that the girls crying somehow made her look bad in front of the teachers. There wasn't a point arguing with her, but I did record her saying racist shit. I never did anything with the recording, I just couldn't believe my ears. Principal Hillbilly really didn't want anything "Mexican" in the yearbook even though that was pretty much our entire demographic. Oh, and anime. Yearbook girls liked anime a whole lot, and Principal Hillbilly flipped out over anime, too. So now some shitty whitewashed yearbooks for school year 2020-2021 are sitting on shelves somewhere at both the Hummingbird Academy and its corporate office. I made sticker pages of the deleted sections for my yearbook students, and we all agreed not to get involved with anything related to yearbooks ever again.

Part 28

(March) I become the off-brand counselor

Yearbook class was over, and I awarded my girls 100 percent. When I logged into those specific classes, I saw there were journalism lessons I was supposed to teach along the way. Oops. Principal Hillbilly never told us anything about our jobs. We were warned that the corporate HR lady was coming to talk to us soon, and she had interest letters we needed to sign as the contracts for next year were fully prepared. Mr. Dutch confided in me that he was not going to sign up for another year, and I told him I didn't think I was going to either. I figured I'd just job search over the summer vacation while still getting paid. I went back to mindlessly giving 70 percent to all the students assigned to my classes, and otherwise waited out the clock on the remaining school year. While yearbook class was over, my yearbook girls still talked to me daily. Sometimes we'd occupy the small group classroom, and I would simply listen to their challenges and successes. More students started asking if they could join our support hour for pandemic fatigue, and teachers started recommending that more students yet stop by to relieve their frustrations. Principal Hillbilly found out I was spending an hour a day checking in on student mental health, and began sending me students who came to school smelling like marijuana instead of immediately dismissing them back home.

Professional Development became extra boring with my mind nearly made up not to return next year. I warmed up to the idea of a chill job search with money coming in from summer vacation pay. Principal Hillbilly, now vaccinated, delivered a PD in person. She brought the English and History department into the small group classroom, and left the Math and Science department on the floor to supervise the students clicking away in the computer lab. By now, a quarter of the student body had returned to campus. The PD was some nonsense about becoming a more functional team, and the activity had us writing and acting out a script where we plan a birthday party. Mr. Pecker turned on his creativity and started writing a script that eventually annoyed Principal Hillbilly because the party planning elements meant to showcase our individual strengths quickly descended into opportunistic murdering of each other. Mr. Pleats and I kicked back and talked about sports, his dog and his girlfriend's career. Principal Hillbilly also checked out, and scrolled social media on her phone waiting for us to finish our oversimplified team building assignment. Halfway through PD, we heard Ms. Catgastro's bloodcurdling scream.

Two boys on the floor had been mad dogging each other the entire week up to now. One boy had been coming to school in person for several weeks, and the other had only recently shown up. Apparently they belonged to rival gangs, and had past conflict involving drugs, girlfriends and stolen property. The boy better known to us had always been soft spoken, respectful and work minded. Even though he wasn't an English student assigned to me, Mr. Pecker was cool with me walking him through the English essay back when I was more enthusiastic about doing so. The recently enrolled boy made a triggering comment from his computer seat, and the boy we already knew sprung up and unloaded punches onto the shit-talker. That was the part of the fight where Ms. Catgastro screamed loud enough for those of us in PD to hear. Mr. Dutch and Mr. Spudspank responded quickly, and when the rest of us exited the side classroom they had already separated the boys. Mr. Zenslack ate a sandwich. Still, the boys were yelling threats at each other from opposite sides of the computer lab. Mr. Spudspank was doing his best to calm down our familiar student who was now wielding a knife, and Mr. Dutch was calmly blocking the unfamiliar student each time he tried to lunge out of the corner to continue the fight. Mr. Zenslack cracked open a soda. Shit-talker was gushing blood from his nose. Principal Hillbilly, to her credit, bleated out for Ms. Moon or Ms. Catgastro to call 911 instead of just gawking. The rest of us evacuated the other students from the building, and stood around the gas station with them until the police came and took the two boys off campus.

In the immediate aftermath, Principal Hillbilly demanded we get the spooked students back to work before anyone from corporate arrived. Since a few of the students couldn't stop crying, I took them into the small group classroom and began helping them process. They shared that they thought the boys might have started shooting at each other, and believed their lives could have become endangered by guns today. As they spoke, I realized that outcome is a possibility at any school in the United States on any day of the year. I told them the thought of a school shooting scared me, too, but today's fight seemed to be personal between the two boys involved. Before long, we played music and invented silly dances to make each other laugh. Of course, Principal Hillbilly shoved her head into the room and demanded we get back to computers and act like a violent outburst hadn't just traumatized everyone. The corporate spin job included an email to parents about heroic teachers swiftly evacuating the student body as soon as the fight started, and blaming the tempers of the two boys on pandemic fatigue. The email said teachers would receive additional training on deescalation strategies within the next week. When next week came, Principal Hillbilly told us about all the asses she kicked while in high school herself, and how she always let the other student with whom she had beef throw the first punch so she was protected from disciplinary action. Deescalation training over.

I started applying for jobs when I realized HR lady's interest letter (which I signed) meant next year's contract was going to be offered to me before this year even ended. That meant I wouldn't have the summer for my chill job search. Arizona struggles so much retaining teachers that the contracts become a challenge to beat. If a teacher quits then the school can charge them a penalty and also add their name to a database other schools look at before making hiring decisions. So I applied for some lame case management jobs thinking I could secure employment and avoid signing a contract for school year 2021-2022. From the lame case management job, I figured I could conduct my chill job search during the low effort training weeks that always come with those lame case management jobs. I wrote a resume that misrepresented my frequent job hopping by just absorbing multiple shorter employment stints into my few longer employment stints (and I can't recommend this strategy enough, I've committed resume fraud the last few hires and never been caught even with supposedly enhanced background checks). A supervisor from a lame case management agency called me and asked if I could come in for a late morning interview next week, and at first I told her I couldn't because of my school schedule. Then I thought how ridiculous was responsibility in this situation, and said,

"Actually, I'll just tell my principal I'm going to traffic school or something."

"OK, great!" Said the supervisor from the lame case management agency.

"Not that I'm a dishonest employee!" I added to cover my willingness to lie to my employer.

"You're off to an amazing start…" Groaned the supervisor.

Part 29

(April) I write 200 credit slips

The job I interviewed for at the lame case management agency involved writing outpatient referrals for children whose parents brought them into clinical care with behavior concerns. This job was nearly identical to a role I left over ten years ago. Lame case management jobs involve endless paperwork and accruing an uncomfortable level of personal liability since the children in care are always in crisis. If a crisis goes south, really south, then an auditor will step in and come up with a report of times the case manager missed an opportunity to recommend a therapeutic service or a month went by without a proper home visit. I knew I didn't want to return to this kind of work, but could accept the job if doing so meant not signing up for another year at Hummingbird Academy. Then I could just conduct my chill job search during the training weeks while also drawing summer vacation paychecks owed to me from Cactus Academies. The supervisor who scheduled my interview turned out to be a young woman, and was accompanied by another supervisor who was also a young woman. I wondered if I would have been their boss had I stayed in this line of work the last decade, and flawlessly answered their questions about mental and behavioral healthcare. Eventually they asked me stupid questions like, "Report on a time you had to use extra professionalism."

"Extra professionalism?" I clarified, "Professionalism isn't like guacamole where you keep adding more." This moment broke the facade for me, and I couldn't help but laugh at the remaining dumb questions. Especially with us all sitting there wearing masks. COVID-19 changed the world, and there we were pretending extra professionalism was an important skill. I thought my change of demeanor tanked my interview, but the young women called and offered me the job during my immediate drive from their office to my school. I accepted on the condition that we could delay my start date until after high school graduation. I didn't want to incur the penalty for breaking my current teaching contract.

When I walked onto the floor at Hummingbird Academy, I aggressively humped Mr. Spudspank's computer monitor in victory while horrified teachers and students watched. I whispered to him that I got a new job, and danced around the room repeating the news for all the other teachers. I let the students know "traffic school" went well, because I didn't want them to know I hated fake teaching and thought their freebie high school diplomas were a waste of their time and mine. A boy looked up from the sexy music video playing on his smartphone, and asked me, "Sir, do you know what's a WAP?"

"Yes, and turn your computer on and get to work."

After I completed my proctoring sentence wandering around the room redirecting students off smartphones and then writing their bathroom passes (where I'm sure they continued using their smartphones), my mind drifted to how much time my yearbook girls wasted this year not completing their core classes. I considered students other than my yearbook girls who also spent significant time talking to me about their hardships this year, and how not having a high school diploma at 19 or 20 years old was holding them back from working on more productive pursuits. Mr. Pecker and Mr. Spudspank, the most serious teachers on the faculty, complained at times that they thought Ms. Moon siphoned her favorite students off their classes and assigned them to herself. Or took students who were close to finishing a class so she could steal the credit for awarding credit. I sat at a computer, and with some network searching, confirmed for myself that Ms. Moon's process was to acquire students from two groups, those who weren't making any clicks and those who were making the most clicks, then outright award course credit. No wonder Ms. Moon presided over a clique of students who behaved saccharine sweetly toward her. So far this year, Ms. Moon wrote over 175 credit slips. For comparison, an actual content teacher who was ethical all year, like Mr. Pecker or Mr. Spudspank, wrote about 25 to 50 credit slips in the same time. That's a healthy mix from the small percent of students working at school and that majority of students working from home. I decided if Ms. Moon was fraudulently graduating the students with whom she shared close relationships, and also pulling names of students working from home at random just to curry favor from Principal Hillbilly and gain accolades from corporate, then I was going to at least do the same for my handful of students who worked on the yearbook or otherwise won my respect.

I called a small group with Santiago, Diego, Fernando, Maria, Sofia, and Luz, and told them that every student at the district schools got to pass last year with the grade they already earned before COVID interrupted the final quarter, and that was advantageous over the charter format where the abandoned classes rolled over. I also told them that the district schools did away with D's and F's this year, officially the first full school year burdened with COVID, among other accommodations not available to charter students. For example, some students in district schools just gave up school completely because they were satisfied with C grades (earning 70 percent without even needing to click on a web page). I said despite these facts, I still thought the students in the milieu before me were painfully lazy in regard to their academics, and capable of more learning than which they currently aspired. Having said that, I told them I was going to pass them out of all four years of English high school. They cheered and expressed how awesome they found me. I assured them my actions were shameful, but not more shameful than the fraudulent system with which we were all imprisoned together. I said making an incomprehensible number of clicks toward a freebie high school diploma was a waste of time, and I'd rather relieve them of as much of that burden as possible. I told them I could do this free of personal risk because I wasn't returning next year, and I'd rather they move on with their lives, too. I added that the best course of action would be for them to attend community college, but go ahead and submit all the English courses to me regardless of having clicked on everything or not. I would manipulate the outcome. I communicated a similar message to my students working from home.

Without even an attempt to disguise my surplus of credit slips, such as slowly dropping handfuls of tunnel dirt into a prison yard to avoid suspicion, I shoved over 200 credit slips into Principal Hillbilly's box all at once. In the next Professional Development, she shined the spotlight on me and started a slow clap for how much I "stepped up" and helped students finish their remaining English classes. The more serious teachers were horrified, and asked if I was worried about a state audit discovering I oversaw students finishing multiple English courses in a single day. I shrugged and reminded them that my new job started the Monday after graduation. Ms. Moon quietly raged that my credit slip tally eclipsed her credit slip tally, and that nobody clapped for her shenanigans. Eventually, my legendary scam or legendary mental breakdown became known as the "Fire Sale" and students who weren't assigned to me asked for my favor by name.

"Mister!" Shouted a random student, "Hook me up with your Fire Sale!"

Sometimes a consistently ethical teacher came to me, and sheepishly asked if I could offer the Fire Sale to the remaining low credit earners from their courses lest they not qualify for next year's merit raise.

"Hey man," Said Mr. Spudspank, "So I have this nice kid working from home, but his Internet isn't reliable, his computer is full of viruses, and he hasn't really gotten anything done all year..."

"Say less, my dude." And I expanded the Fire Sale to Science, Math and History.

I probably hold some kind of multi-disciplinary record for awarding high school credit in Arizona.

Part 30

(May) I end the school year

Nobody benefited more from the Fire Sale than a deceptively older looking Freshman who was tall, lanky, lazy, unkempt, and only interested in his budding rap career. His name was Ben Bustamante, but he went by his rap handle Lil' Bus. While he never completed schoolwork, talking to him revealed a hidden intelligence. At the end of the year, when I was more popular than ever thanks to the Fire Sale, I strolled back from a jaunt to the gas station with my fresh cup of coffee in hand.

"Hey Mister, let me get at your coffee!" Suggested Lil' Bus.

Now, nine out of ten times that would be a no, but something about Lil' Bus's entitlement impressed me so I handed over my coffee purchased only a minute ago.

"Thanks! I've never tried coffee before!" Laughed Lil' Bus as he lifted my coffee to his lips.

Lil' Bus took a sip, and his face involuntarily scrunched up for nearly 30 seconds before he regained control and composed himself.

"Blech! God, that's disgusting." Concluded Lil' Bus as he continued to stare at my coffee. He removed the lid to better inspect the liquid that just made him retch.

In a moment of glory, Lil' Bus shouted, "But Lil' Bus ain't no bitch!!"

He chugged my entire hot coffee in one fell swoop. This student impressed me more than any other student to date, so I promised I'd spend the entire final month of school supporting his rap career. Our epic partnership was born.

For my last month, I almost exclusively sat in the small group classroom helping Lil' Bus get his social media platforms set up correctly, listening and advising on his raps, and making sure we hyped his music to as many potential fans as possible. I did my best to organize Lil' Bus flash performances for students and the other teachers to enjoy. Eventually we raised Lil' Bus's profile enough that he was always called by his artist moniker even by Ms. Moon and Ms. Catgastro. When Principal Hillbilly asked me what the fuck I did all day, I told her I was starting a school-wide beautification project called Trash Patrol. Lil' Bus and I spent half of his academic session picking up garbage around the school (brainstorming), and the other half of his academic session recording and uploading new raps (spitting and spreading the fire). Lil' Bus selected royalty-free beats, and confidently laid down genius rhymes like, "I'm from Maryland / Where I fucked ten bitches named Karen!" Unleashing Lil' Bus was probably my second greatest COVID-19 year accomplishment.

The last day of school was anti-climatic. We teachers showed for the final grading day before graduation, and sat in an empty computer lab same as we did that first day of school and so many subsequent days thereafter thanks to COVID. Ms. Moon strutted around patting herself on the back for edifying young scholars. Mr. Dutch worked on math hobby projects for fun. Mr. Zenslack took a nap. Mr. Spudspank congratulated us in earnest for doing the best we could with what we had to work with this year. Ms. Catgastro refused to wear her mask now that students weren't in the building. Mr. Pecker organized all the amazing supplemental materials he made this year so he could expand on them next year. Mr. Pleats sat and chatted with us about sports, his dog, and his girlfriend's career. And I texted back and forth with Lil' Bus who was at home writing raps. Mr. Spudspank thought Principal Hillbilly might muster a few inspiring words to close out the first full school year of the pandemic, but she only emerged to say she was headed to the corporate office and none of us were allowed to leave until the exact minute our shifts were scheduled to end. Her corporate business was to figure out what to do about chairs in the graduation celebration since the hotel required social distancing and suddenly our school produced way more graduates than anticipated. As soon as Principal Hillbilly's car left the parking lot, I dipped out the back. Mr. Dutch caught me while also dipping out the back, and we hugged away the trauma of having spent an entire school year at the Hummingbird Academy. As soon as I got home, I knew I wasn't going to leave again for the graduation. The idea that I supervised students clicking through a canned curriculum was humiliating enough without also celebrating the fraud. This all started with me wanting to be a real teacher, and now the dream felt dead. Soon, I'd be working at a lame case management agency and starting over from nothing. I turned off my phone, and drank a beer. I incurred a $500 penalty for ditching the graduation ceremony since apparently my participation was a contractual obligation. Hilariously, a statewide audit conducted over the summer did produce a professional consequence for Ms. Moon, who resigned, but I was long gone. Principal Hillbilly denied ever supporting the Fire Sale for students not committed to their clicks.

I FINALLY DATE A HOT CHICK (BUT THERE'S A CATCH)

Part 31

I meet the woman of my dreams

Once I was vaccinated, I wanted to do something about my pandemic fatigue and depression. I had avoided bars and restaurants to do my part to slow the spread, and also because I took offense to my Qanon coworkers visiting bars and restaurants as aggressively as possible; like I had to stay home extra hard to make up for their super spreader events. I suppose we were all virtue signaling for our respective camps. Anyway, as I ventured out to restaurants I live around, but never tried, I found most of them disappointing. The burgers and steaks I had been cooking at home in my cast iron skillet were superior to the food for which I had to pay more money. Obviously having the company of a young woman would elevate the experience, so again I started swiping.

I matched with a redhead named Melody, who immediately messaged me an initial comment with solid effort behind it. My profile mentioned pandemic fatigue and depression, and she said she could relate. I was vaccinated in an early priority group because I was a teacher, but she had not yet had the opportunity because she was working from home selling cellphones and accessories. She owned the fingers at the other end of those "How can I help you today?" chat bubbles when you log onto a cellular provider website. She still asked me out, and proposed a walk with both of us wearing masks. I was comfortable with this idea because in her photos she wasn't that pretty. Her profile pic was a low angle selfie that gave her a slight double chin (as we all would have from that position) and her other photos were grainy and taken from a distance. I was actually pleased that she was chubby and frumpy because after such a long time in quarantine I was no longer confident in my first date abilities. As shallow as it sounds, I thought of this coming walk as a practice date or dipping my toes back into courtship. She didn't make me nervous.

Imagine my surprise when I got to the trail head and saw a tall and statuesque red haired Amazon warrior stand up to greet me while wearing a short flowing red skirt and black boots. Oh great not only was she toned and beautiful, but she had inches on me. Now I felt awkward as fuck. I said hi and introduced myself, and she did the same. I asked if she were ready to walk, and she obliged. We started down the path that had traffic on one side, and wash on the other, and battled a wind that really picked up while trying to get to know each other. I remained acutely aware of her intense physique as I blandly asked how the smartphone customers behaved for her today. Her piercing green eyes, peering out from above her cloth mask, clued me into her disappointment with me and this get together. After we walked a ways down the path, she stopped, said she had enough, and that she wanted to head back. I obliged, and we turned in place and started backtracking over the quarter mile we just came. No loop, no finish, no sense of accomplishment. Just a straight line and back.

Back at the trail head, she warned me that she wasn't looking for a relationship right now, but appreciated the opportunity to get out of her house. She said her friends urged her to try online dating, and she felt compelled to let them know she did, and it didn't work. She added that she didn't want to lead me on, and that with the pandemic and a recently discarded seven year relationship I probably couldn't count on her for future dating. I let her know, as an experienced online dater, that her etiquette was not yet calibrated to the expectations men carry into these dates. I assured her my self esteem was sufficiently developed to survive this being our only encounter. I closed with, "Melody, you can't hurt me." I would come to choke on those words.

On my way home, I stopped at the grocery store to stock up on goodies for the weekend. A teacher buddy who knew I had a date texted me for an update, and I answered that she was a hottie, but not interested in me as evidenced by shit conversation and apathetic body language. But before I could complete the checkout, Melody texted me to say she had a wonderful time. What the hell? By the time I got home, I had received a photo of her 16-bit old school video game paused on a screen before her bare, outstretched legs and the beer she was drinking. Her visible ankle tattoo was an eight-bit ape tossing barrels off a construction site. On second thought, I believed I might be in love. As I put groceries away she asked for help on a part of the adventure for which she was stuck, and so I booted up my copy of the same game and recorded a video aid. We engaged in this back-and-forth for hours, and had the most amazing time. The encore date completely obliterated the actual date. Melody told me, "I'm sorry if I was awkward earlier, you made me nervous and I was just button mashing to get through it." We planned a second date.

Part 32

I never see this coming

Going into the second date, I had mixed feelings and confusion. She said all that shit about not wanting to date, but then she followed up with fun and games all night. She was into all the old school nostalgia I was, and also super hot! Super, super hot. I decided to take her at her word that she was just nervous when we met, and ignored the fact that a woman that beautiful should not be at all nervous around me. I was going to proceed like we were into each other, and met her at a fancy restaurant in the Foothills. When we linked up in the parking lot, all the awkwardness from our windy wash walk returned. I held her hand to stroll to the front of the restaurant, but she reacted poorly and I let go. We sat down, and the conversation didn't flow. She did remove her mask, something she hadn't done on the first date, and again I was struck by her unparalleled beauty. She put her mask back on to find the restroom, and seeing her walk away was the first time I noticed dat ass. I would go to war for dat ass. Melody was gorgeous, awkward, and in her downtime enjoyed classic gaming. Damn, what a woman! "Too bad she's still not into me," I thought.

After dinner, we put our masks on again and walked to the cars. Similar to the first date, I thought this was it. Even if she wanted to play video games tonight, I figured there wasn't much point to going on new dates if they are this painful for her. I've never met such a socially anxious hot chick. With about ten steps left to her car, she un-looped one side of her mask from an ear and then did the same on the other side of her face. Her mask fluttered in her hand all the way down the side of her curvy body. I thought, "Oh my god, her mask is off! We're on." I quickly tore off my mask right before she tossed her arms around my neck and gave me a quick, uncoordinated peck. "Goodnight!" She said, "I had a really nice time." I tried to kiss her again, but the landing was awkward because, while she didn't entirely resist, her body language was tense and her lips remained tightly shut. Okay. I didn't understand her, but she was amazing.

Finally, at the third date, we hit some kind of stride. The banter over text leading up to the third encounter had been flirty and fun. Not only was she gorgeous, but incredibly witty. I enjoyed her humor and learning about her interests. She sent me photos of stacks of books she was reading, and art and keepsakes with which she decorated her house. Melody had a little cat with a funny name who wore bow ties and hats. She was into DIY projects around her home, and crafted a comfortable backyard with lights and a fish pond. The third time I saw her was at a music festival. The event was socially distanced, and lightly populated. We had a big bench to ourselves to watch both the performers there in person and the performers beaming in from other locations via a screen service. She was wearing tight jeans, a white blouse, and wedge shoes that put her even higher above me. This time she held my hand with confidence, but when we walked around to visit concessions or see lights I almost felt like our height difference made her my babysitter. My sexy hot babysitter.

The making out was fire. Back in our bench, we became completely entangled and kissed, and kissed and kissed. I had my hands all over those long legs, which sent me directly to heaven. She stopped once, and warned there were things about her I might not like. She went down a list that included veganism, being staunchly child-free, and smoking weed. What she said exactly, was, "I smoke weed. A lot of weed. Just so much weed, and I'm not going to stop." I guess she thought that would turn me off because I am a certified substance abuse counselor, but I had a raging erection and couldn't care less. She added, "My dad is a hermit who lives in the desert and grows his own weed, and in a week or two when the crops are ready I will go and help him harvest his yield." As we continued to kiss she mentioned more things like her eight-bit ape tattoo not being a tribute to late eighties classic gaming, but representing her favorite party drug. Nothing swayed me to stop kissing her. We walked back to our cars in the dirt parking lot after the concert concluded, and my rock hard erection showed real staying power. She felt my nether region, and quipped that as a high school teacher I must have experience hiding boners at the chalkboard.

Before I even got home, she texted me that she would like to go on a day trip next weekend. Of course I agreed, and fell asleep happier than I had ever been after just three dates. I felt so good having met an intelligent, funny, and beautiful woman who not only didn't flake, but actually came up with exciting plans of her own. She had interests and hobbies, and was including me and choosing me. Come to think of it, I never had this before. The fourth date day trip was a dream. That's all I really need to say about it. The day trip was perfect in every way. Well, she did break her favorite water bottle, but that provided me an opportunity to purchase a new one and ship it to her overnight. She texted me immediately after checking her mail, and said my gesture was sweet. She also said she thought our fifth date should be the "streaming and chill" consummation of our new relationship.

Part 33

I fake an entire month

"Jason, I have genital herpes."

"I'm sorry, what?" I asked Melody. The first time we were about to have sex, she sunk into her couch, the light leaving her eyes, and she eked out some words.

"I have to tell you something. I have HSV-2. Genital herpes. It doesn't affect my life in any way other than these moments right now. I have had lots of boyfriends. Too many boyfriends. And I've never passed herpes to any of them. Guys don't care, but do what you will this information."

My head was spinning, but I knew I had to muster a supportive response of some kind because this woman I've been falling in love with did something brave. I told her, "Thank you for telling me. Let's not have sex tonight, but if we keep seeing each other then it shouldn't be a problem."

We just watched TV and then I went home. I was almost in a car accident when I, deep in thought, ran a red light. Herpes? How many boyfriends? Guys don't care?? I felt like less of a man not wanting to go through with the sex if in her experience most guys didn't care, but a thought materialized that would nag at me in every future interaction with her: I also didn't care if we were going to stay together. We would just be the cute herpes couple. But if she infected me, and then dumped me, I'd be going back into the wild worse off than before. She would still be an insanely desirable woman, but I would be a social pariah. I'm like the very bottom of the middle echelon of men women want, and having herpes would drop me down to the dirt. I'm guessing the men who didn't care just didn't think that far ahead. Or were desirable enough that they could comfortably drop a rung on the hierarchy. Could I really trust the most exciting woman to ever pay me any attention to stay with me forever? And what about all that weird shit she warned me about? Herpes. Weed. Vegan. Child-Free. No.

I knew I needed to end things, but then I remembered my other childhood trauma. Girls in middle school ridiculed me for wearing basic white underwear even though I had no control over purchasing my clothes, and they wouldn't even know what I had on were it not for boys from the locker room telling them. I figured since Melody and I weren't going to have sex, but we did make out like crazy, I could finish my social experiment of revisiting my childhood trauma as an adult. How would Melody, the sexiest woman I knew, react if she undid my pants and caught me wearing the undies that have been socially unacceptable since middle school? I picked up some briefs from the dollar store, and shoved the stupid colored boxers I'd been begrudgingly wearing since sixth grade way aside in my drawer. When I put my new underwear on the next day, I found them very comfortable. They didn't bunch up like boxers, and after about an hour of wearing them they conveniently shrink wrapped to my body. When I got to Melody's house after work, I predicted she would just break up with me and I wouldn't have to even do anything. She opened the door, we kissed, she plated delicious food she made, and we sat on the couch. All this was amazing, and everything I ever wanted, but fleeting because she had a communicable disease that scared me stupid. I made sure I wasn't wearing a belt when we started fooling around on her couch so my pants would slide down in the heat of the moment. With me on top of her, I did get lost in the passion and forget about the experiment, until she paused, peering over my shoulder, and asked, "Do you wear tighty whities??"

With her dress hiked up to her waist, I could see she was wearing very sexy black panties. I thought of a response, and told her, "You know by now I'm pretty basic." She then asked a follow up question, "Every day?" I hesitated, and she giggled up her own answer: "That's a yes!" I shrugged, and told her, "Look, in our relationship you're the sexy one. You're the half wearing sexy underwear." She thought about it for a moment, then said, "Okay! I can handle that," and she pulled me back into making out. For some reason, the whole exchange made me incredibly horny. I think that's just an unfortunate side effect of childhood trauma. We both stripped down to our underwear, but eventually I rolled off her, not wanting to take this further because of the herpes (ugh life is not fair). Sitting there with a hard on that my new underwear could barely contain, she asked if I wanted her to take care of me with her mouth. I begged her to do so, and she ripped the waistband of my briefs getting my dick out. I'm not sure you can call what I got a full blowjob, because after just three sucks I came like a fire hose. I sat there in what I thought was pure bliss, but then she opened me another beer and I was even better. Not only was Melody selfless and sexy, she solved my childhood trauma by accepting me even while I was committing a massive social faux pas. Even though doing so killed me, I left that night without getting her off.

The next day Melody texted me to consider that while she has genital herpes, she is still in fact a person. When we met that night, she said she talked about what happened with her therapist. She said she didn't feel secure in our fledgling relationship because while we were hot and heavy, we stopped before having sex which was a "micro-hit" to her self esteem. At this point, I hadn't done all the genital herpes research I have since (like so much research since). I didn't know that after a positive person makes a disclosure, they expect the other person to just accept that they, too, will probably get infected. And that's the cost of having a rewarding relationship. Hell, half the posters of /r/herpes think having herpes makes them cool. They wear the confirmed diagnosis like a badge of honor commemorating their success in love and sex. Here I had been thinking that her disclosure meant we should just date without sex, and continue doing our cute outings safely out of concern for my health. Nope. So I was about to break up with her, when she proposed what her therapist recommended, "Why don't we take sex off the table?"

"For how long?" I asked. "A month." She said. Great! I reasoned I could live out my fantasy of having a wonderful, caring girlfriend for an entire month and then end things.

Part 34

I do the right thing (eventually)

I started living two parallel, but very different realities.

When I was with Melody, all I could think about was how lucky I was that she wanted to spend her time with me. Melody was a queen. We went to antique shows and she haggled for more of the knickknacks she liked to display in her house. We went to arcades and played pool and racing games for hours. We competed in mini-golf and, while she was fiercely competitive, she wasn't obnoxiously competitive. She also won 90 percent of the time because she was incredible. We affectionately held hands for all the walking we did. We embraced at every greeting and goodbye. There was never a question of with whom I would be spending my time after work. I felt so good having a person. Never in my life had somebody chosen me over and over again. Every time. I did not have to compete for her attention. We were together, we seemingly loved each other, and I was happier than I had ever been in my whole life. I love you, Melody. I loved you then, I love you now, and I will love you forever. My actions, behaviors, and obviously these inappropriate words do not properly show love, and I am intelligent enough to know how horrible I sound throughout these stories. Even the number of times I described your physical attractiveness is at odds with how I really feel. As the flawed human being I am, I love you, your personality, your kindness, your grace and charm, and only wish you great outcomes and happiness. Not that my wishes matter. You do not need them, and they are worthless to you. I am scum, and you are rain.

Unfortunately, when I wasn't with Melody all I did was search the Internet for herpes information. I learned everything there was to know about herpes. HSV-1 is a virus that primarily affects the mouth and face, but can also affect genitals after oral sex. HSV-2 is a virus that primarily affects the genitals, but, in very rare cases, can also affect the mouth and face. HSV-1 causes an initial outbreak on the lips and then hides somewhere in the brain stem where the body's immune system can't detect it, and can reactivate at any time for the rest of a person's life. HSV-2 causes an initial outbreak on the genitals, and then hides somewhere at the base of the spine where the body's immune system can't detect it, and can reactivate at any time for the rest of a person's life. Herpes has no cure or vaccine, but medication management can lessen the severity of symptoms. Severity of symptoms will also lessen over time as the body adapts to playing host to the virus. A person with herpes is most infectious when there are visible sores, but asymptomatic shedding means a person can be infectious even without visible sores. Men catch herpes less than women due to women having more of an exposed entry point for infection. About one in every eight men have herpes, and about one in every five women have herpes. Some people do not ever show symptoms. Sores are viral fluid filled vesicles that burst and crust over. The scabs fall off and do not leave scars. When triggered, herpes travels via the nervous system between the skin and its hiding place. Like COVID-19, you can't predict how your body is going to react to the virus. Obviously being healthy bodes well for the experience. Melody and I never really talked about her particular infection, but I knew she lived with genital herpes for ten years when we met and that it was a sensitive topic. So I felt a lot of shame spending every morning sipping coffee while scrolling through gross pictures of active outbreaks.

During one of our last dates, we visited my apartment's swimming pool. To date, it's the only time I've ever used my apartment's swimming pool. When I watched her emerge from the steps, coming off the ladder like that famous movie scene, I knew I had to tell her. She was dating me with intent, and I was dating her with deception. I couldn't get on board with the risk. Even a condom only reduces the chance of infection by 30 percent because it doesn't cover all the areas from which the herpes virus sheds. And even though she is only contagious a few days a month, which amounts to a two to five percent risk of infection a year, I knew if I caught herpes and she dumped me I would never find love again. On the flip side, she would definitely survive a breakup with dumbass Jason. That night our hot and heavy making out lead us to stripping down to our underwear again, and in the throes of passion I blurted out, "I would love to tear off your panties and fuck the shit out of you!" This time she paused, and acknowledged the flaw in our relationship, and urged me to finish my thought, "Buuuuut...?" I caught myself, and said, "But, well, we still have a couple days left on our no sex therapy assignment." Melody sighed, and said, "I wish you'd fuck the shit out of me."

That night she handed me a letter she wrote at home documenting all the things about me she loved. I cried while reading her note alone in my apartment. Today, seeing it hits differently, but we're not there yet in this book.

Part 35

I lose the woman of my dreams

I didn't want to pull the trigger. Until Melody, my longest lasting relationship was only eight months. If you read my first book, you know that relationship ended because of a single deal breaker, too. This felt different because the deal breaker was something she couldn't control. Melody and I had only been dating three months (barely, if you add up the initial match, texting, and the time between early dates), but I knew I would miss her for years to come. She started including me in bigger and bigger plans, such as an intended double date with her boss and his wife, followed by an intended dinner with her brother and step-mom. I wanted all those events to happen so, so badly. Nobody had ever, ever included me in their life like that. But at the same time, going through with relationship advancing plans and then breaking up with her would be unforgivable. I was not going to embarrass this lovely soul. With regard to the end of our therapy assignment, Melody told me she was scouting out places where we could be under the stars when we make love for the first time. I predict nobody will prioritize intimacy with me like that again.

I opened Melody's photo on my tablet, practiced putting a condom on a stubbornly soft penis, and tried jerking off while the anxiety of knowingly exposing myself to an STD fought against the process. Task failed. I just couldn't make progress. If I thought about going through with the sex then I was basically left without the ability to get an erection. I was going to have to separate from a goddess, go back to my lonely life, and die knowing... "Most guys don't care."

"If only I was one of those guys!" I thought to myself until I noticed some red bumps on my scrotum. "What the fuck is this??" I panicked. I contorted my body into every possible position to gain a better view of these bumps I was seeing, and then took a hundred cellphone pictures to look again with various magnification and clarifying filters. I had a week long panic attack, and exposed myself in public several times (always checking, always checking) until I realized that until now I never noticed my raw skin after shaving away pubic hair looked tender, bumpy and red. When all was said and done, I had spent $120 on STD tests that came back negative. Living like this wasn't fair to her or me. I wished I wasn't scared, but, I was, and couldn't cajole away my concern: "I'm going to catch herpes, she'll leave me, and I'll be unlovable forever."

I barley answered Melody's texts the weekend my panic attack reached its peak, but she thought we were going to the movies that Sunday night. She was vaccinated now, and wanted to do more even though she had taken plenty of risks to date me while vulnerable. I called her, and forced the words out of my mouth, "I love you, but herpes is a deal breaker."

"You don't want to see me again?" Quivered the voice belonging to the woman I love.

"I just don't see a path forward," I told her, explaining how the virus is always in the back of my mind, and causing me daily stress.

She said other things, but prompting her to say, "Please delete any pictures you have of me," was another self inflicted dagger in my heart.

There was no reason for the woman I love to be feeling this way. There was no reason for us to not be in the honeymoon phase of a real relationship. I let her down, and this was game over.

Most guys don't care. Herpes. Weed. Vegan. Child-Free.

She hung up the call because she couldn't collect herself. She also texted me at 2 a.m. and thanked me for letting her be a part of my journey.

All class.

Dumbass Jason.

2021

I GET REAL BAD DEPRESSION

Part 36

I'm too sad to catch them all

For the last five years, I've relentlessly played a single mobile game: The one where you catch the pocket monsters. Yes, that one. And I've spent money on it, too. What can I say? The nostalgia factor got me. I knew my vulnerability so I avoided downloading the app during its early hype. Then I did, and I've been committed ever since. My legacy-interest is fueled by how many hours I played the original games alone in my room when I was a teenager. And watching the anime. And collecting the toys. Not so much the cards. At least I can say I never carried around reams of cards or went to card shops to battle other nerds. Actually, now that I typed that out I probably would have been better off engaging in some of the social aspects of this franchise. In the recent past, I've had my friend code listed on my dating profile, and planned dates around playing this game. I've been offended when I've shown up for one of these catch-the-pocket-monster dates, and my companion had to "re-download the app" since they "hadn't played in awhile" or offended when they were done after ten minutes and expected us to do something else in addition to that for which we met up. I always ended those dates and continued playing by myself. This game served as my primary coping skill through so much intense heartbreak and psychological pain. Until Melody's genital herpes disclosure, pocket monsters cured everything. The one time I reached out to her and checked if we could be friends, and she told me she was in a happy relationship and didn't want to hear from me, became the time I finally lost interest in my hobby.

My first account (yellow team, by the way) kept me busy during my tenure at the group home. Our group home was between two prize points which to this day are ranked very highly for engagement with my original account. I could walk to the church down our actual street or the video game store where our adjacent street touched our major road. Some of the boys who lived in the house would play with me each time I needed a break, and others wished they could, but the typical group home resident's phone was a busted device with no service so they could only play at places like the video game store where WiFi was available. Catching pocket monsters was largely a bonding activity for me and my wards, with the exception being that gifted young man I told you about earlier who was frequently left waiting on the porch after school. He needed us to get back from the park to unlock the door so he could start his homework, and sent many angry texts saying so. During this time, the manager of the nearest group home for girls was a worthy rival. She made special trips with her van full of foster teens just to attack and hold the prize points by us for which we felt ownership. The boys, after noticing a defeat, would start hollering to me that we had been bested, and off we charged toward the church or video game store to right the wrongs.

When Esperanza Siempre issued me a dedicated work phone, I immediately registered my second account (also yellow team). There was so much more I could do with two accounts. Since my main responsibility was facilitating IOP with Old Alpha Male, I frequently left my office to walk all over downtown carrying a phone in each hand. With two accounts I possessed more power to attack and hold prize points, and I could trade my captured pocket monsters with myself in hopes that the trade would be blessed with a rare power up. My second account quickly became as strong as my first account. I could hold onto prize points longer because I had two sets of teams to leave on guard. Doing that deterred unknown rivals more than just either account on its own. I also went through the process of nominating our building as its own prize point, and opened the app one glorious day to see the moderators finally approved Esperanza Siempre. I was beside myself, and spent the whole day engaging with my personal prize point. I was very proud that my own photos now existed in the augmented reality for everybody playing. Curious about my excitement, Strange Hippie

Lady registered an account and was quickly hooked. Catching pocket monsters together raised my tolerance for her poor decision making around her upstairs program for girls. I showed Businesswoman that Esperanza Siempre had its own prize point knowing she wouldn't quite understand what she was seeing, but she interpreted our logo existing as interactive in a mobile game as positive advertising and thanked me for pursuing the honor. The most difficult challenge after leaving Esperanza Siempre was adjusting to the loss of my work phone and losing daily access to my special prize point.

The first time I looked for pocket monsters inside my little brick apartment building, I was delighted to see I could reach a prize point if I squished myself against my bedroom back wall and wiggled around enough that my character in the game would take an extra half step toward the street. Due to GPS drift, I sometimes rebooted slightly out of range, but I could close the app and try again and appear where I needed to be at least 75 percent of the time. For awhile, I managed my two accounts by toggling between them on my personal phone, and eventually ordered a tablet to migrate my account from Esperanza Siempre. I could again play two games simultaneously. When COVID-19 struck, the game released some stay-at-home accommodations which included doubling the radial range around prize points. This meant I was no longer confined to my back bedroom! I think I was sitting on the toilet when I first noticed the difference. I bought another tablet, and registered a third account (still yellow team), and spent all my time that summer rocking unemployment and leveling up in my favorite game. I posted all three friend codes on the usual websites meant for gaining connections, and enjoyed exchanging digital loot boxes with new friends from all over the world. When I masked up for my daily walks, I threw my devices into a pocket monsters themed backpack and took them with me. Even if the tablets didn't have a wireless connection, the gyroscopes could still track my steps and then I would get credit for the distance the next time I reunited with an Internet connection. The lockdown months would have been a lot lonelier without my pocket monsters.

By the time I worked at the Hummingbird Academy, I was on my fourth account (my only red team affiliation). Instead of a tablet, I bought the same phone I was already using, but didn't activate the duplicate. I just used the additional phone as another WiFi dependent device. I started the process of nominating the Hummingbird Academy as its own prize point, but abandoned that effort when I gave a second thought to how stupid a fake school was with no real classes. I concluded that the pocket monsters were better off not having my crappy charter school cheapening their digital neighborhood. While "teaching" in Hummingbird Academy, I could only engage with a smattering of prize points attached to fringe churches that looked more like trailers. I persevered, but often fantasized that COVID never hit and I was still enjoying the better in-game amenities I had at Esperanza Siempre. I could have gone my whole life not knowing Businesswoman was a lunatic if she never had the global pandemic with which to gaslight and abuse her staff. Pre-COVID Businesswoman was preferable to Principal Hillbilly. But in good times and bad, my favorite mobile app, the game where you catch pocket monsters, was always there for me. My dad is an accomplished player, too, and these days playing together is probably our most consistently shared activity.

Whether the pocket monsters can trounce my depression this time remains to be seen.

Part 37

I'm sad and still loathe behavioral health

After I unburdened myself from the indignity of "teaching" at a fake school, and let a shocking genital herpes diagnosis and its aftermath run my heart through a blender, I really didn't want to start this next job at the lame case management agency. When I say I was shocked, I mean I was shocked to my core. After breaking up with Melody, waiting a couple months, asking her if we could be friends, and being told no, that she was already in love again, I literally couldn't focus on anything other than sadness. I vacillated between comforting myself that I did the right thing avoiding a potential genital herpes transmission and then torturing myself with the very low probability that I would have received the infection if we took every precaution and did everything right. I finally settled into my conclusion that while the risk of infection was low, it was never going to be zero, and the fact that she moved on so easily probably meant I was right to assume we would not have been together forever. But that shit still hurts. Immensely. Although I escaped catching herpes on my mouth or genitals, I think herpes will always hurt my heart. I didn't have to clock into the Hummingbird Academy and always be walking, so maybe I could take the transition into the lame case management agency as time to heal. At least I was allowed to sit down.

Before I tell you exactly what happened at the lame case management agency, I need to provide some information on the industry. Behavioral health jobs are abundant and low value. Every behavioral health agency is always hiring case managers. Always. Case managers are what make the scam work. You really don't want to work as a case manager unless you're intending to quit after the training period. The training period is always long and arduous, because these agencies are very top heavy. So you typically have weeks and weeks and weeks of training in quality management and data validation and health care infrastructure in preparation for the thousands of documents for which you are about to become responsible. Again, this work is absolute hell and spreads worse than herpes. However, there's that ramping up process where you are only responsible for training followed by a small stretch of time before your caseload swells to an unmanageable size. If you just need a quick buck, go ahead and accept a case management job and then quit the second your caseload exceeds what you were originally promised at your interview. All the agencies boast that their case managers aren't overworked, and they're all lying. There is no case management agency that can keep staff, because the work is absurd and success is not achievable.

So the way this Arizona Health Care Cost Containment System (AHCCCS) scam worked at the start of my career twelve years ago, was that the government gave a huge amount of money to the Regional Behavioral Health Authorities (RBHAs) that then split up the money between the networks and agencies. The networks and agencies either rendered services for mental and behavioral health or subcontracted with specialty providers (like Esperanza Siempre and its juvenile drug counseling). Within this system, case managers were responsible for "encountering" that money. Sometimes an agency would accidentally describe what its case managers did as "billing" for services, but the money was already received, so really its case managers were only "encountering" for services. If an agency didn't encounter all the money it received from the RBHA then it would not get the same amount the next year. If an agency really fell short then it might even be responsible for paying back money. Obviously this all means case managers are bullied and whipped about billing (encountering). Every agency I ever worked for (and I worked for a lot because I could always quit and start at a new one) had some preposterous billing expectation for its staff. Sometimes an agency was transparent and said "bill five hundred dollars a day" and sometimes an agency tried to soften the blow and said "encounter 25 units a day." And then there was some conversion formula for how much time and money was recorded in a unit. The system was convoluted the whole time, but I didn't know how much worse it had gotten until I joined the lame case management agency, but more on that in the next chapter.

Agencies treat their case managers as the lowest of the low. Case managers meet with new clients, write their service plans, and send their referrals. Case managers then follow up to make sure clients are meeting with their therapists and progressing toward their goals. Case managers also have to write crisis plans, daily progress notes, monthly progress notes, cultural discoveries, participate in Independent Education Plans (IEPs), semi-annual and annual updates, transfer summaries, closure summaries, professional staffing notes and a thousand other types of notes that are always due and due again. Forget to do one thing one time? Congratulations, you're the scapegoat the second anything goes wrong with a client. And some clients are always in crisis because there just aren't enough counselors, therapists, hospital beds, and group homes to go around. The newly graduated therapists come in through the agencies that accept AHCCCS (Arizona's medicaid) and then leave for private practice the moment they gain experience. After many years, I discovered the secret to success in these case management jobs was to learn the difference between a good lie and a bad lie. Obviously lying about a client's treatment details is a bad lie. But lying about how much time you spent on a billable or encounter-able task is a good lie. I simply got into the habit of always lying about how much time I spent encountering money for the agency, which then spared me that aggressive bullying and whipping from management so I could focus on actually helping the handful of clients who stood to benefit from a therapeutic working relationship with me.

The very first time I was hired into a behavioral health job as a case manager, the supervisor leveled with me and said she wasn't going to check references or worry about my lack of experience because she just needed five new staff to start immediately to avoid a fine from the state for being dangerously understaffed. She even suggested I bring a book because I wouldn't be able to do anything until I was trained, and she didn't know when she could offer training. I still hadn't been trained by the time I received my first client, and, when the grandmother called me and said her adopted grandson (my client) had come home from school and provoked all the neighbors into hating her by ringing each doorbell along his walk, I asked her what the heck she wanted me to do about it. "I don't know," She thought it over, "Could you just come talk to him?" That was the first time I threw a little client's folder into my backpack, set my staff magnet to "out of office" and headed over to a home to talk some empathetic sense into an angry, depressed or otherwise traumatized kid. Ding dong ditch and I became buddies, and according to his grandmother he really benefited from my mentoring. This scenario played out over and over again, and my niche became the aggressive young people other case managers wanted to avoid. For awhile I enjoyed the challenge, but I possibly liked being away from the office more.

So the way I settled into working my first case management job was probably the only way to approach any job that truly doesn't give a fuck about you. I tried to help kids as much as possible and then lied about billing because the success metrics were simply not achievable. For example, you're supposed to write progress notes for every phone call you make. And billing a three minute phone call legitimately takes ten to fifteen minutes to properly document. You will never make your daily quota that way! Just spend 45 minutes helping a kid like Ding Dong Ditch and then write a progress note saying you were with him for 90 minutes. My bosses were always happy, my clients were always happy, and I was always happy-ish. But the fraud and abuse was never more evident than when the CEO of my first agency handed my boss a corporate referral. The supervisor who hired me had no choice but to hire this asshole whose grandmother was a revered judge. Asshole was never going to show up for work, but he was going to draw income as an indirect way for our CEO to donate to a political pet project: Arizona's Bicentennial Celebration. My supervisor was upset because asshole's salary made her unit look like its overall billing or encountering was down an entire person (because it was). Asshole walked around the office once in a blue moon, hit on women, and offered to take me to strip clubs. At a strip club, Asshole encouraged me not to work very hard because, according to him, our CEO liked to laugh about how little he paid us.

Behavioral health is a joke. Do not work as a case manager unless you are in on the joke!

Part 38

I'm sad my coworkers are miserable

I started my job at the lame case management agency. Predictably, it was lame as shit. I walked into the morning meeting, and two staff were already there; a young man and a young woman. They were still green about working, and in the immediate past experienced unfounded excitement when they got hired out of college for this $18 an hour job. For them, case management responsibilities took about five and eight months, respectively, to break them. So I walked into that morning meeting, and the two staff already there immediately hushed their conversation in progress. Understanding what was happening, I assured them, "Don't quiet down on account of me, I'll be quitting in a few months, too." They both breathed a heavy sigh of relief, and unloaded how much they hated their jobs. The young woman already had her next job lined up and was waiting on the background check, and the young man didn't give a fuck about his next job. He was just done. My new boss entered the room, and we started the meeting. My new boss was one of the two young women who interviewed me, but not the one who originally called to schedule the interview. She was the other one, the one who asked me about my extra professionalism. Quintessa was quirky and kind, and a case management savant. I actually came to enjoy working with her. I partly stayed as long as I did to offset how many staff Quintessa hired that immediately quit after training.

Ironically, reporting to work at the lame case management agency was like stepping into a COVID-19 time machine. When I left the Hummingbird Academy, we were basically done with COVID (even though COVID wasn't done with us). At the lame case management agency, we had 50 percent of the staff working from home and absolutely no clients in the building. We also had to wear masks at all times. The break room was a step up from the teachers' lounge, but plastic shielding was everywhere so if I ever ate lunch on site (I didn't) I'd be separated from others by my own little terrarium. Aside from those two coworkers who quit during my first week, I got to know most everybody else over video conference only. Seemingly, the vast majority of my coworkers were female again. I missed the camaraderie of having "bros" like Mr. Dutch and Mr. Spudspank, and tried to befriend an older guy named Horatio. I enjoyed being able to come and go as I pleased again, a freedom I didn't have while stuck at school all day, and brought Horatio some snacks from one of my many trips to the gas station. "Did you buy too many?" He asked, not understanding my offer of friendship. I tried to bond with Horatio many times, but was never successful. My man was all business.

Quintessa invested a lot of time showing me the new case management software. All the basic forms I had come to know from working case management jobs for time immemorial were represented, but now with extra steps. So, so many extra steps. I remarked that she was too young to know how much simpler documentation used to be, and I swore billing and encountering never used to take three screens, a second monitor, and several popup confirmations. The software also offered gaping holes for user error. For example, you could choose the correct "place of service" (home, school, clinic, community) above and then below when selecting your billing code accidentally choose the incorrect "place of service modifier." Like, why can't the software stop the user from making a selection that is in conflict with another selection on the same page? Why can't the software warn you that the place of service conflicts with the place of service modifier? Every time a staff made this mistake, an audit person sent an email with all the supervisors CC'd and requested a correction. Corrections also took another several pages and wasted half an hour to complete. I used to get so frustrated with the correction emails before I became an electronic medical records ninja like Quintessa. The most horrifying change to the convoluted world of behavioral health was that the Regional Behavioral Health Authority split into seven separate health plans under AHCCCS, and all of them made unique rules and regulations. Never before in this job setting did I have to consider different courses of treatment for my clients based on health plan affiliation. Only because Quintessa was nice, I decided to change my quitting strategy from the end of my training to the end of my 90 day probation.

What else? Well, my lame case management agency was basically a front for drugs. The legal drugs like anti-anxiety medication and anti-depression medication. So with COVID protocols, I didn't get to roam the community mentoring young boys like Ding Dong Ditch as much as I did in years past. I mostly met with exasperated parents over video conferencing software and then set up telemed appointments with our two psychiatric doctors. Because the psychiatric doctors were so in demand, I befriended the women who managed the medical appointment schedule so my clients always got seen with priority standing. Since I went to the gas station multiple times a day, I always brought something back for Brie and Leah. But, like everyone else at the lame case management agency, Brie and Leah quit before too long. In fact, one of the two psychiatric doctors quit, too. The Great Resignation that rolled behind the COVID pandemic was washing away all my colleagues faster than I could get to know them. Hilariously, my lame case management agency was still conducting new intakes even though there were no staff to pick up the new cases and no counselors, therapists or doctors to see the new clients. Coworkers like Horatio were overwhelmed with quadruple the number of cases promised by our job description. I would have been equally overwhelmed, but I told Quintessa I would quit if my caseload rose above what she told me at my interview. I felt guilty, but, hey, in my line of work we're always counseling clients to "maintain good boundaries." Even though Quintessa was a supervisor, she managed a boatload of cases to prevent her sinking staff from drowning. I respected her more for her effort.

I leaned into the staffing crisis, and warned my clients as I met them that the state of behavioral health services was bleak. I let them know, accurately, that they would be waiting a long time for any counselor, therapist or psychiatric doctor. I encouraged them to call 911 if faced with a real crisis, and said the police might get them into a facility quicker. Unfortunately, COVID dropped a big burden on mental health in the community, and I had a lot of teens in the hospital for suicidal ideation and drug overdoses. Like I said before, these situations were where I put my full effort. If a teen landed in a facility close enough for me to visit, and the facility allowed visits (not all of them did during the pandemic), then I would go and bring some of my young adult curriculum. We would set goals, make safety plans, and just talk about life. A facility I frequently visited had adults and children sharing a waiting room before admitting the two groups down different hallways. As bad as bed availability was for children, I saw plenty of unhinged adults destroy that shared waiting room. I got used to watching 90's era sitcoms on the wall television while potted plants exploded around me. And speaking of 90's era sitcoms, oh my God the flagship program with the group of young adults living together in New York does not hold up well. Saying this may be in poor taste, but watching episodes sometimes made me want to kill myself, too.

All in all, I flew under the radar, refused to work more cases than what was originally advertised for my position, spent half my day chilling at the gas station down the street, and when I wasn't directly facilitating a video conference spaced out and ruminated on the recently concluded genital herpes saga. I even absentmindedly pulled my dick out of my pants at my cubicle one day to check for viral fluid filled vesicles that burst and crust over. There was no reason to believe I had herpes since Melody and I never did anything more than that blowjob, but I was heartbroken and the idea of herpes infected my daily thoughts. I even started taking an everyday dose of L-Lysine, which is the recommended supplement to boost the immune system, to suppress non-existent herpes outbreaks. Again, I consistently tested negative for both HSV-1 and HSV-2 months after dating Melody, but while working at the lame case management agency I relentlessly thought about herpes and behaved in bizarre ways that acknowledged herpes and my lost relationship. Did you happen to forget, over the course of reading this book, that I'm crazy? I would never bother Melody, or any woman, after she asked me not to reach out again, but I'll always fall into depression and do psychotic shit that's disruptive to my own routine. I also got a hold of some permanent markers and drew herpes all over my penis and groin. Sometime during my STD live action role play, the clinical services director for our lame case management agency found out I was a certified substance abuse counselor. She asked if I would offer a training not just for my site, but simultaneously broadcast myself to all of our sites across Arizona.

I thought, "Hmm. Training case managers and clinicians all over Arizona to provide substance abuse counseling is a good way to fuck things up for Businesswoman over at Esperanza Siempre."

I agreed to train my entire lame case management agency the state over, attempted to wipe off the fake herpes (a struggle because I used permanent marker), and confidently put my dick back in my pants. I decided to change my quitting strategy from the end of my 90 day probation to however long it took to ruin Esperanza Siempre.

Part 39

I'm sad, but my old boss is sadder

I nailed the statewide training. I didn't even prepare that much. That counseling certification program Esperanza Siempre sent me to in Chicago was the most useful piece of training I have ever received. Honestly, I would have liked to go back and redo my group home days with all those skills to help young people seek prosocial replacement activity. A lot of the tools are common sense, so I guess my staff and I achieved the same results with trial and error, but my counseling modality is really spot on. The treatment is designed for substance abuse, but you can replace "substance abuse" with any negative behavior and the remedy is the same. You can't talk somebody out of a destructive habit, but you can help them succeed at goals they find more important up to the point where destructive habits lose appeal (like writing this book instead of illustrating herpes on myself). I facilitated the statewide training from a video conference room, and went through the entire curriculum of which I am certified, with examples from my years of experience. The curriculum used to be a closed curriculum that only those of us with certifications could access, but the licensing body reconsidered this position when COVID-19 triggered a lot of substance abuse, and opened it. The authors made the associated forms available for free online, and only recommended certification. From the pandemic forward, clinicians no longer needed to be certified to use this specific treatment. After my statewide training, I was regarded as my lame case management agency's substance abuse expert and imbued with the ability to train others.

The next meeting I attended was about building an original substance abuse program. I was going to teach classes on site, and my groups were going to be the first in-person service to welcome clients back into the office. Until now, my lame case management agency always referred substance abuse cases to Esperanza Siempre. In fact, until this discussion about offering our own drug and alcohol meetings, I dreaded the day an overdose case might land on my lap. I didn't want to collaborate with Strange Hippie Lady and then appear on Businesswoman's radar. Now I couldn't wait for them to find out why the referrals, at least from the place I worked, dried up. An immediate challenge to my ultimate goal was that I was going to have to work under a big tent. The higher ups wanted me to facilitate a group for 12-17 year old males needing social skills, anger management, and substance abuse recovery. The age range was too wide, and the needs were too varied. Those demographics should have been split into several targeted groups, but executive leadership wasn't convinced there were enough clients willing to come into the building. Somehow I needed to successfully engage with both an archetypal 12 year old wanting to make friends in middle school and an archetypal 17 year old on the cusp of dropping out of high school because he carries a gun and sells drugs (and every type of client in between). Eventually, I got it done. I created an atmosphere where the younger clients were comfortable clowning and asking questions, and the older clients felt good passing down brotherly advice from their own experiences. I couldn't lean too far into seedy topics, but when an older boy needed a private talk I kept him after class. My group was going to be a hit.

Yet another challenge included a partner forced upon me. While Esperanza Siempre had no problem selling me and my former coworkers to the community as clinical therapists, my lame case management agency was too by the book. I couldn't be too upset being relegated to a meager case manager with a counseling certification, because that's what I was, but being paired with a Master's level therapist caused me some concern. Her name was Amy, and she was just out of college and thought she knew more than she did. Amy wasn't ready for that 17 year old tiptoeing the line between staying in high school or murdering a rival gang banger. She was well suited for the 12 year old wanting to make friends, though. My own supervisor, Quintessa, assured me that Amy was there just to justify the billing codes (since we were calling our service "therapy" as opposed to "life skills") and that all the content was still entirely up to me. Amy scheduled a video meeting with me (even though she was only a hallway away), and I tutored her beyond my crash course at the statewide training. I came to respect Amy's skills, and appreciated the artistic activities she showed up with even if making glitter submarine tubes didn't always gel with my memories of how Old Alpha Male used to run a teen drug class. I think Amy came to respect my skills, but several times she scheduled video meetings with me (for the love of God just walk over to my desk) to complain about how I blindsided her with a "totally inappropriate rant about genital herpes" and pressed me on why I needed to divert from the lesson plan and tell all the boys they can still catch herpes while wearing a condom. Well, Amy, that's just good information for everybody to know. My group was a hit.

My hit group grew in popularity enough that the higher ups eventually asked Amy if she would be comfortable spinning off a girls group and she agreed. We parted with no hard feelings, and, again, I think she's a quality clinician. She received a case manager partner from Quintessa's team and I received a new therapist partner from the clinical services team. My new partner's name was Nika, and she was wonderful! Nika was incredibly knowledgeable and talented (like Amy) but also with some lived experiences (like me) that helped keep the vibe closer to what I was used to when working with Old Alpha Male. I think a safe space for sharing, with conversation spoken in the language of the dominant counter culture, makes for a perfect boys group. Having both a rewarding boys group and a supervisor I admired kept me at my lame case management agency for way longer than I had ever anticipated. The clinical services director who originally tapped me for the statewide training, and got the ball rolling on my group, tried to expand my role in the company again and assigned me a college intern. This development was a bummer for two reasons, one, with an intern in tow I couldn't go to the gas station multiple times a day, and, two, my intern was kind of forgettable. Like she literally had no personality. But my group co-facilitator Nika was such a great partner she even took my boring intern off my hands several times a week. For a brief moment in time, I was content doing the type of work I once only did out of necessity while between other endeavors. I also stopped giving a fuck about robbing referrals from Businesswoman. The teens we helped made a greater accomplishment.

My work life was so stable at the lame case management agency that I am pivoting back to trauma and sex for the next five chapters before I tell you about another rage quit. But, don't worry, my contribution to the Great Resignation of 2021 is worthy of the #WorkReform and #Antiwork movements.

Part 40

I'm sad while committing a poop crime

"I got your letter, and I appreciate the apology. I'm in a really healthy relationship with someone I care about a lot. It's best if you don't reach out again. I really do wish you the best."
Melody
September 2021
10:00 a.m. Tuesday

I was still in agony three and a half months after I broke things off with Melody over the phone. I couldn't wrap my head around why she baited the hook so much before tossing in the dealbreaker. When I joined the dating app, I wasn't looking to date somebody with an STD. I've had sex with over 40 women, mostly unprotected, and I've never caught an STD. I tell my dates that unfortunately I can't stay hard while wearing a condom, so if that's their preferred method of birth control we can only be friends. 95 percent say that they don't like condoms either and we proceed to have a great time, and between the remaining five percent half request an STD test and then we proceed to have a great time. I've had two encounters with STDs prior to Melody. There was one woman who matched with me, built up some texting chemistry, and then sent me a pie chart about genital herpes as part of her disclosure speech. I thanked her for letting me know, and informed her I was not comfortable with any amount of risk. She said that's too bad, and moved on. I can't fathom why Melody engaged me on a magical day trip before telling me about her genital herpes. That seemed dishonest and manipulative, yet I still missed her terribly and couldn't focus on my job at the lame case management agency. Oh, my other encounter with an STD was when the health department stuck a letter on my door saying I had been exposed to a communicable disease. I ignored it, but follow up letters arrived at my past addresses including my parents' house. I finally called, got tested, and breathed a sigh of relief when everything came back negative. The clinician said I was remarkable in that I didn't even have cold sores which most my age group had by now. After more than 90 days, I sent Melody a handwritten note apologizing for how I handled the end of our relationship, and let her know the time we spent together meant something to me. I was careful not to sound like I was asking for any particular response, but was truly hoping a friendship might rise from the ashes. Nope. She responded with the above text message, and it destroyed me. Now, I know I am the bad guy of this story. I know Melody thought she would date me as passionately as she could, and then tell me right before we made love that she carried a common virus that is manageable with treatment. From there, I would either reject her or accept the risk of developing genital lesions and continue with a rewarding relationship. My inability to cope with disappointment isn't on her. But I have to be able to get stuff done in a day, and the easiest way to move on from my daily misery to a modicum of productivity is to remind myself she really fucked me over by not telling me from the get go. When I joined the dating app, I wasn't looking to date somebody with an STD.

Fuck you, Melody!

You lied, wasted my time and hurt me.

I started dating again to try and move on. That's what people do, right? And the overwhelming number of dates I scheduled fed my ego. Unfortunately, they were all ridiculously stupid. I met up with one woman from Canada who never went home due to COVID-19. She proposed the venue, and when I got there saw that of course each table was outfitted with old school video games. Melody would have loved it. When the Canadian sat down, she wasn't interested in gaming. She just wanted to shoot the shit about our boring lives and lame jobs. Her job turned out to be triggering for me in that she worked for the evil educational company that created the canned curriculum the Cactus Academies pumped out to its students through five rotten schools. She also made way more money than me, the teacher who had to clean up the mess when students didn't want to spend five hours a day consuming garbage. I unmatched her after the date, but then accidentally rematched with her on a different app. She asked me in good humor if I made a mistake matching the second time, and I lied that I deleted my other account in error. We went out again, but I was more bored than before and did something I never before did on a date: When the check came, I told her what she owed for her half. For the life of me, I couldn't find chemistry again. I went on another date with a successful music teacher. She was teaching at schools before COVID, and then switched to offering violin lessons online. When she arrived at the restaurant, her forehead was oozing pus from a gaping wound. She waited until we were eating to explain that she had some skin cancer removed earlier in the day. Her laughing was so obnoxious that other tables glared at us. This is when I went on the date that opened this book. The date was doomed from the start because as I sat there, trying to feel an inkling of chemistry with this undercut wearing, tattooed, pierced and progressive looking medical bookkeeper, I just kept remembering how I felt being there with Melody. She and I covered a lot of ground in such a short time, and now I was left with nowhere I could go on a date that wasn't ruined by the loss of my best friend and almost lover.

Melody, thank you for wishing me the best.

A bowling alley is about to call security on me for pooping in an unflushable toilet.

I TRY TO MOVE ON

Part 41

I answer a paramedic's night call

Sometime after Melody's final text (which I never answered), I came home from work and laid on the floor to sob. Just a full on ugly cry. I was sort of impressed since I couldn't remember the last time I cried, and had been beginning to think I might be a sociopath. No, I think most of us non-baby boomers who can't get anywhere in the United States despite "doing everything right" in regards to college and career are just dead inside. But after learning from the source that Melody moved on from me in an instant, and my life was once again joyless and terrible, I collapsed into the fetal position and cried my eyes out. I was happy for Melody, I didn't want her to suffer, but despondent that nothing wonderful ever works out for me long term. I received a single text message while blubbering on the floor, but didn't look at my phone until I had no tears left to cry. Eventually I glanced, and saw that the half Mexican half Iranian woman ten years younger than me who had been texting me halfheartedly since we matched on the dating app had asked, "Wyd?"

Farah lived in a different town that was 90 minutes away from me, but worked as an EMT linked to a hospital right by where I lived. She worked a grueling night shift three nights a week and then had four days off. Obviously I thought she was gorgeous when we matched, but her inconsistent texts were consistent with the behavior of the most punishingly beautiful women on the dating app. They'll match with me, but the conversation will peter out and die almost immediately. I was surprised Farah revived a dead conversation, and answered her inquiry about what I was doing with a simple comment that I was home this night about to drink a beer and go to bed. She wrote back that she would come join me for a movie, or even half a movie if I needed to get to bed, but that she wouldn't be drinking because she needed to be ready to pick up her kid from the baby daddy in the morning. By now in my life, I didn't let random women I'd never met in person before come over to my apartment for the first meeting, but I had literally just been a pathetic puddle of depression.

I sent Farah my address, and composed myself a bit. My face was puffy from crying, so I splashed cold water and also drank some. I decided to put on a pair of boxer shorts and a tank top since that was what I would be sleeping in, and waited nervously for this sexy stranger to knock on my door. But she didn't knock. Instead, the stream of "OK I can't find your complex ugh" and "my phone is about to die while I'm lost" texts started piling up. I called her and got her voicemail with no rings. "Well," I thought, "That was weird, but predictable." I cracked open the beer I wasn't going to drink until I had company and turned down my covers so I could climb into bed before too long. Except a final "I think I'm here" text rolled in so I stood in my doorway until I saw a curvaceous EMT dressed in black leggings and a tight black top coming up my stairs. I greeted Farah, but she rather shoved past me and found an outlet to plug in her phone. She plopped down on my couch, as something recently added to one of the streaming channels advertised itself on my TV, and asked, "Is this what we're watching?" I sat next to her, said we could look for something good, and sipped my beer.

Farah talked a mile a minute. I was happy to have bubbly company, in stark contrast to how I was feeling, and also happy that I didn't have to entertain. If she just wanted to unload her thoughts while her phone charged and then leave I would have been perfectly fulfilled. She stopped many of her stories in the middle of the plot to check her phone over in its little corner of my apartment before returning to the couch and starting a completely new story based on whatever random friend's text she just read. I figured I had nothing to lose, and took Farah's hand while she was speed talking. She gently squeezed my hand back, and never missed a beat sharing her story. When she wrapped up what she was saying, she commented on us holding hands, and teased, "Look at you making a move!" I smiled and shrugged, and started kissing her. She kissed back for awhile, then stifled a little laugh and added, "Now you're kissing me, too??" Farah told me she thought I was too inexperienced with women to try anything because of how much I told her about catching pocket monsters. She said she lost interest in our conversations since they were mostly screenshots from my mobile game accomplishments.

While Farah and I kissed on my couch, my steel beam of an erection freed itself from the fabric fly flap of my boxer shorts and made itself known. "Goddamn!" Shouted Farah, "You've got a boner just from a minute of kissing me? Are we going to have sex??" I said, "That depends, do you have genital herpes?" And she clapped back, "Why the fuck would I have genital herpes?" Good enough for me. I removed her clothes, and, yep, those were two pierced nipples. The little barbell kinds. As soon as I entered her I felt the sensation that I was about to cum. The realization hit me that I had been making out with Melody for so long, but stopping short of actually doing anything due to my fear of genital herpes, that I was tightly wound and ready for release. I asked Farah if I could finish inside of her, and she gave her blessing. I apologized for how quickly that nonsense had unfolded and resolved, and she said she didn't care and that she didn't think she'd be having sex tonight at all. I didn't need long before another steel beam of an erection appeared, and this time I was able to fuck Farah as long as she wanted and in multiple positions. When we finally finished fucking, I asked again if she thought she had genital herpes, and she responded with annoyance, "Why do you think I have genital herpes? I get free STD tests at work." I apologized again and asked if she wanted to meet up for a meal later in the week, and she raised an eyebrow as if I missed the social contract for tonight. To her, this was just a hookup and we weren't going to ever go on any dates. I asked if we were ever going to have sex again, and she said sex again was within the realm of possibility, and she did enjoy herself. She also said not to be offended if she never called. When I got dressed to try and walk her to her car, she stopped me at the top of my apartment stairs and said this is where we kiss goodnight.

I never heard from Farah again, but thank God for her. I could look around my little brick apartment again without seeing lingering signs of Melody's ghost.

Part 42

I team up with super women

I met two (hopefully) lifelong friends when I needed them the most. The best metaphor I can think of to describe discovering Marketplace Madison on a dating app is panning for gold. There's a lot of murk and mire to sift through with a few treasures mixed in if you're patient enough. When Madison and I matched, I struggled to comprehend what she was trying to tell the world with her emoji driven profile, but she further explained to me that she was looking to date multiple men without a hierarchy. She had done the "monogamy thing" and encountered a few "hobosexuals." That is an otherwise homeless man she then had to take care of in her house. She went on a date at the start of the pandemic that never ended because the man said he lived with his geriatric aunt and uncle, but couldn't go back to them because of their comorbidities. He also bought a ferret while living in Madison's home rent free, and then sold her the ferret when he moved out. The alternative, he threatened, was letting the ferret linger in pain without a necessary medical procedure he couldn't afford. Yeah, I guess I'd be done with dating men exclusively, too. Madison and I met for pizza, and, while she was beautiful, my first and a half impression was that she was weird as fuck. She stuck to her guns on the non-monogamy thing, not that I was trying to persuade her otherwise, and talked about not believing any one person could meet all of her complex mental, emotional and sexual needs. I was jealous of my recent ex, or she-who-will-no-longer-be-mentioned-by-name, having already found her way into a "really healthy relationship" while I was out dining with a dating anarchist. Madison insisted on paying the check, and even though we drank beers with our pizza, we moved down the street to a better bar to upgrade our drinking.

Talking to Madison was mentally stimulating in a rare way. She was very politically progressive, but worked in an industry I think our country would be better off without. However, from her position she believes she could be a force for positive change. I'll just say she does something in large scale land management that from my vantage point makes purchasing or leasing a home more difficult for the little guy (like me), but, according to her, she wields her influence and expertise to assure the capitalists that they can grow their success by actually offering better deals to the common consumer. Then again I really don't know what the fuck she does. But she is obviously very intelligent, and confirmed by me to be generous to a fault. When I attempted to hold her hand as we strolled between destinations, she switched our linkage to a gentle arm-and-arm arrangement I liked better. Madison possesses a mystique of strength and femininity of which I cannot help but be attracted. We kissed at the end of our first date, and, like the improvement she made to our stroll, her kissing style was also an upgraded experience. I'll accept that she can work her magic to improve the rent crisis facing people like me. Madison graciously kept hanging out with me, and offered that we could "date" inside her definition until I met somebody more monogamously aligned with my goal. At that unspecified future point we could transition to a platonic friendship. Maybe because past recent dates discouraged me from sending pocket monster related screenshots, I spent several weeks knowing Madison before learning she shared team affiliation in my mobile game. Hell yes! Now I had a friend for life who could partner with me in excursions related to my favorite hobby. Marketplace Madison, as I came to think of her and describe her to my social circle, became my best friend. I may not be her best friend, but she is mine. She was also the genius who turned me on to erectile dysfunction medication as a way to defeat my inability to have sex with a condom. Note- She didn't have sex with me, she just handed down the tip (no pun intended). Madison was instrumental in helping me conquer the bout of depression that triggered this book, and making me feel like a stable and healthy person again.

Beulah also performed a miracle for my self esteem. Unfortunately for the annals of history, I can't go into as much detail with her story because we worked together at the lame case management agency, and the circumstances of our meeting are too tightly woven into the job for which she still excels. To obfuscate her identity away from the possibility of anyone recognizing her would also diminish the meaning of our bond. So I'll say this about Beulah. She is charming, capable, kind, intelligent, sweet, effective, hilarious and super hot. We didn't exactly have an enduring reason to consistently cross paths on the job, but were drawn to each other and invented the reasons needed to collaborate. I was crushing on her for awhile, and didn't suspect any reciprocal feelings until she gave me her personal phone number under the guise of addressing an insignificant business matter after hours. I took a chance on some sexy banter, and like a lady boss she told me this night was my only chance to impress her with a dick picture – and that she would never ask again. Under pressure to deliver, and motivated by a steamy selfie she included with her request, I inflated my boner as much as possible and recorded myself masturbating. Beulah approvingly said, "Not bad." And we became work spouses. I never symbolically married a work wife or even took the concept seriously before, but suddenly sharing a deeper connection with a coworker made wage slaving much more tolerable and even enjoyable. We constantly texted, talked about our day, supported and encouraged each other, and she playfully, but firmly, rejected my every effort to sleep with her. Thanks to Beulah, I can point to at least one beautiful woman from the last ten years and say I created a meaningful connection without the Internet paving the way. Although I'm long gone from the lame case management agency, Beulah and I still talk almost every week. I couldn't have asked for a better ex-wife.

"I do not recommend sending a photo of your penis to somebody at work."
- Marketplace Madison

Part 43

I star on a huge streaming service

The Tucson film industry had been in remission for years until suddenly one of the main three streaming services decided to film a pilot in the Old Pueblo. I saw the open casting call for background actors in several places, but ignored all of them. The potential series had something to do with a getaway driver for an emerging crime syndicate in the 1970's southwest. Somehow a cool car was supposed to be important, too. The show sounded interesting, but I figured the production was already inundated with college students wanting to be famous. And a leading man like me doesn't audition. Eventually my mom forwarded me the casting announcement from the newspaper at a time when I wasn't doing anything else, so I broke out of apathy and sent in the same best photos of myself I curated for dating profiles. After I sent in my photos, I caught that I didn't answer the written questions and responded again with all the information filled out correctly. With some embarrassment after my inability to follow simple directions, I let my mom know I answered the casting call and then forgot the whole thing happened.

About a month later, while wandering the hallways at the lame case management agency, I stopped in front of Quintessa's doorway and read an inbound email. "Huh," I said as I opened a message from the production studio. "Looks like the streaming giant wants me for its pilot, but I'd have to stay available for COVID-19 testing multiple times this week and next."

"Make it work!" Shouted Quintessa. "You have my permission to make it work."

With Quintessa's blessing to put my real job on the back burner, I sat at my desk and filled out additional forms from the show. I needed to upload my COVID vaccination record and enter account numbers to accept direct deposits. As I read over the generic contract, I quickly calculated a big pay day. The show was paying me $100 per COVID test, of which there were many, $50 for an hour wardrobe fitting on Saturday, $250 for an eight hour shoot the next Saturday, and $30 an hour overtime every hour thereafter. My thoughts raced like a 1970's getaway driver: "Why the hell do I hang out at my regular bullshit job if TV pays this much?!"

I was nervous walking onto base camp for the fitting. I felt like the crew from Hollywood was going to judge us local Tucsonans chomping at the bit to feel special for once. I followed the signs with arrows reading "Background Actors and Extras" and made a mental note to correct anybody at my real job who accidentally called me an "extra." My paperwork clearly said "background actor" and that must be more important. Then I came to a barrier that read "No Background Actors or Extras Beyond This Point" and took personal offense. Suddenly, a fancy woman with an apron full of sewing supplies introduced herself to me and pulled me into a huge dressing trailer. From there she and some of her staff pulled clothes for me, and also warned me that everything was vintage and to do my best not to damage any of it. I tried on several suits and some lounge wear from the 1970's. I learned I was a background actor in a lobby and bar scene, and was going to look like a guest of the hotel. They took several photos of me in each outfit, and I really wanted the tight colorful pants and open silk shirt they put me in around the midpoint of my hour. Unfortunately, the fancy woman and her staff settled on a simple brown and orange suit. While I wore the suit, they marked areas that needed modifications with pins before bagging it all up and labeling with my name.

I hesitated letting myself get too excited until after the fitting, thinking that at any moment I could receive an email saying I was no longer needed. When the last work week at my regular job leading up to the shoot reached the point coworkers started sharing plans for the weekend, I said shit like, "While you guys enjoy your time off, I have to go to work at my other job filming your next season of high quality entertainment." My deadpan coworker Horatio asked me, "Are you in the Screen Actors Guild?" And I didn't know if that was a real question or a sick burn. The email with my final itinerary didn't arrive until after 10 p.m. the eve of the shoot.

The complicated shoot was taking place in an old hotel downtown. Downtown itself was taken over by trains of trailers related to the filming. Some of the trailers were just incredibly posh mobile bathrooms. Hollywood is amazing! I showed up ready to work, but most of my day was just waiting around. I sat in a tent with other background actors, about 20 of us, and eventually a group of ten (not me) were called away to get dressed for a construction site scene. I waited longer. The group of ten that included me was finally called to dress, and I received my wardrobe from the fitting. After I put on my suit, we were told to grab lunch from catering and keep waiting. And my God the food was delicious! We got to eat several times that day (be mindful of wardrobe), and everything was delicious and best of all free. I love Hollywood! Looking around, most the women background actors were either young and beautiful or old in a stereotypical way. The men had a widely different range. We all looked pretty whack. When the fancy woman came around to check our final looks, she told me I could skip hair and go straight to makeup. I guess my real look is anachronistic for the 2020's, but right at home in the 1970's. We were finally called for the hotel scene.

Masks off! Masks on! Masks off! We never got a break from taking off and then putting on our masks. At least Hollywood takes COVID more seriously than the high school I recently quit. When I finally made my way on set with my other background actors, an assistant director grabbed both me and a young woman and said we were going to be a married couple. He pointed out across the dimly lit hotel lobby that led up into a bar full of fake cigarette smoke, and directed us to stroll the length of the floor, walk all the way behind the bar, and sit to the back left of some main characters and order drinks from the bartender. He had us go through the motions for him once, then asked my TV wife, "Miss, are you comfortable with him touching you more affectionately?" She consented, and I put all my online dating experience on display. We then shot that same scene over and over again for hours. Another assistant director got into a disagreement with the first one over my glasses, and depending on with whom I last spoke I had to take them off or put them back on. I got nervous that I was going to get a problematic reputation when that second assistant director saw me wearing them again, took my photo, and sent an inquiry to the show's creator. He who directed two of the last three installments in the world's most well known epic space franchise definitively decided my glasses stayed on.

Eventually, the creator showed up to direct the next scene. The series star also showed. The star took the same breaks we did, and the female background actors absolutely swooned over him. I watched from a distance, and again lamented not pursuing an acting career. I thought I was more handsome than the star other than he was way taller than me. I guess that's an important difference. I thought back to the lame case management agency, the Hummingbird Academy, and Esperanza Siempre and realized I was meant for bigger things. Well, I did help a lot of kids. I guess that's an important accomplishment. But damn I could do that anyway if I were a famous movie star! My TV wife and I started spending break time together, and I let her know how much more enjoyable this whole experience was having a partner. The other background actors who had to open doors, light cigarettes, walk or pour drinks or whatever by themselves didn't look like they were having as much fun. In our second scene, we had to react to a brawl and a chase through the lobby. If the pilot ever makes its way to streaming, you will definitely see me at the side of your screen. I was the closest background actor to the camera when the star and the female lead ran away from a huge charging bad guy with a bloody nose.

I went home that night and updated my resume to include professional actor.

Part 44

I meet a Queen

Surprisingly, I haven't been on a dating app in the last five months. This is probably my longest detox since I first started using them, and I owe my absence to an incredible woman named Sky. She was my last match and as of writing this we seem to still be going strong. Her profile was unique in that there were clues she held several prominent positions in the community, including a professional headshot that looked like a stock photo from a corporate image library, but she also came across as shy and reserved. We set up a date without too much back and forth banter, and she was down for a simple walk in the park. Because the day of our date coincided with a community event in my favorite mobile game, I half jokingly told her I would bring enough devices for her to join in on the fun. She said I should go ahead, and that she was open to trying anything. I brought my two phones and two tablets, and when we finally met I had to hurriedly put a tablet in her hand and tell her to keep tapping on the final boss that spawned a minute before she arrived. I'll never forget her completely reasonable reaction after several minutes of this activity, "Why is this fun to you?"

Despite Sky's inexperience with pocket monsters, the reward associated with her win was a one-in-20 chance. I tried to communicate just how rare was the outcome on her screen, even showed her the difference between my other screens, but she remained unimpressed and shrugged. We walked and talked, and Sky still seemed shy and reserved. I even felt like she was a little scared of me. The park darkened and depopulated quickly so I asked if she was hungry, if by chance a brighter venue might salvage the evening for her. We walked to a pizza restaurant and sat outside because of her ongoing concern for COVID-19. Unfortunately, nighttime construction along the street meant sitting outside was noisy and distracting. I felt like the date was fizzling fast, not in an awkward and regrettable way, just that the likeliest outcome was not seeing each other again. Fortunately, the pizza was delicious and the beer was relaxing. Unfortunately, Sky came out as vegetarian and a non-drinker. Yeah, the last of the date swirled the drain. I ate my whole meat pizza (of course) and Sky ate half her vegetarian pizza and asked for a box to take home. I enjoyed the meal with a well put together woman, and would always have the special pocket monster she caught for me. When we walked back to our cars, I had no intention of trying to steal a kiss. However, Sky gave me a look that made me think doing so was OK, and I quickly kissed her goodnight. Sky grabbed me, and kissed me way more deeply than I had her, all while still holding her pizza box. Damn, what a woman.

Sky and I went on at least two dates a week. Usually a weeknight date when her little kid was with the baby daddy, and then a date on Sunday when she was able to get a babysitter. I really liked her a lot, but always felt like she was lukewarm about me or going out with me because there wasn't a compelling reason to dump me. She never seemed enthusiastic about me, that is, until the end of our dates when we would spontaneously make out for an hour and leave everybody else in public uncomfortable. We did some really cute activities like visit art galleries and go rollerblading. I never tried to escalate things past kissing because she still seemed shy and reserved the majority of the time, but I really enjoyed the consistency of us getting together. I tried to avoid comparisons to she-who-will-no-longer-be-mentioned-by-name, but unfortunately she and Sky shared a unique trait (not genital herpes). In no way did I seek out this feature twice, but they both have beautiful red hair. During those early dates, I felt a small amount of anxiety wondering what would happen if Sky and I accidentally crossed paths with my ex and her new boyfriend, and the ex confronted me over auditioning a replacement or something totally not apt but hard to explain away as coincidence. I considered breaking up with Sky because the more time I spent with her the more I came to know her as the kindest and most vulnerably honest woman I've ever met. I felt like a jerk in comparison. Although Sky makes me want to be a better man, I've still taken all these horrible actions chronicled in this book.

So why is Sky so amazing? I'll tell you with a funny story. Shortly after we went rollerblading, Sky told me that we were caught in the rumor mil. Some of her students saw us in the skate park, and captured clandestine photos of us that they then shared around social media. I was the mystery man with Sky, who was their revered mentor and life coach. Sky ran a STEM camp for teens and was heavily involved in local politics. I've only seen this personality type once before. In college, one of my buddies presented as shy and reserved, but he also worked as a successful stand up comedian. Once he was on stage, or in his element, his personality shifted to a hilarious headlining funnyman. When we were back to hanging out, he shifted back to shy and reserved. Similarly, Sky skirted around a genius level intellect while with me and then went off to cultivate computer coding and robotics abilities in wayward teens who would then be employable for life. Sometimes her teens competed at hacker or battle bot events in Las Vegas and won cash prizes or scholarships. I guess teaching teens to make pocket monsters is more fun than playing with pocket monsters. Sky had her own building with classrooms, but also supervised teams of highly qualified instructors that visited schools. If you read my last book, you know I used to become jealous when dating women more important or successful than me. Not anymore. Sky is a queen, and I am completely in awe of her. We started having ridiculously hot sex.

Approaching six months, I can't explain how I've consistently enjoyed two dates a week with a beautiful woman who is talented and compassionate beyond measure. Sky once answered my direct question with the response, "Well, I can't just do work and mom things all week." She is no longer that shy and reserved around me. After we saw a recent movie, just to make a date out of going to the cinema (the flick was simultaneously available on streaming), she came out of the theater ranting about Hollywood once again ruining a good idea with the white savior trope. Her passion surprised me and also turned me on. Then another time, she became flustered when a news article about successfully harvesting pig organs to use in humans didn't start a wider social conversation about no longer eating pork. And sometimes she will just break down and cry about climate change. Fuck it, I cry, too! Billionaires enslaving us in a capitalist system to kill the planet is worth crying about. If more people were like Sky then humanity and the world wouldn't be in such dire straits. Damn, what a queen.

My ongoing time with Sky is now my longest and most rewarding relationship.

Part 45

I rage quit for fun

Back to this $18 an hour bullshit for a minute. The Great Resignation had a horrendous effect on the mental and behavioral health community, the effects of which were especially devastating in my lame case management agency. While aspiring to help families suffering from mental and behavioral health challenges is a worthwhile pursuit, I've previously detailed for you how the government and private systems work to steal as much money as possible in lieu of actually helping anyone. I once worked with a homeless teen who wanted $500 to go into the same halfway house her mom lived in while trying to get clean. Sounded good to me. This young girl eschewed coming into clinics, and previously refused any and all form of counseling through my lame case management agency. I filled out the forms for that once a year cash assist we're allowed to use to help our families, but our psychotic new site director rejected my request and said not without convincing the girl to accept wraparound services from us. I told the psychotic new site director that my homeless teen wasn't interested in a therapist, and was only agreeing to speak with me in regard to the very specific type of help for which she was asking (cash to join the halfway house). The psychotic new site director, who I'll call Karen from here out, said this plan was terrible because my homeless teen would need another cash assist the next month. Nope. I said the halfway house uses its resources to help the residents get jobs after getting them clean, and then everyone pays their own rent each following month. Unmoved, Karen wouldn't accept anything short of forcing this girl to come into the office and sign up for a weekly counseling service with us. When I went back to my teen with the news, she hung up on me and disappeared forever.

Now let me take you on a quick semi-related tangent. When I was still a group home supervisor, I met a case manager from this lame case management agency named Vera. She was chubby, but cute, and super passionate about working with teens. She was too young to know she couldn't really make a difference while with a lame case management agency. Every now and again, a resident in my group home had behavioral needs that were case managed by Vera. So we worked together on and off, and naturally started banging. Vera made weird requests (besides asking me to do her in the butt) such as wanting the ability to stop into my apartment when I wasn't home and tend to phone calls or emails while she was out in the community. Sometimes I relented, and sometimes I didn't. There was a time we had satisfying sex, but I refused to let her spend the night when she wouldn't stop propagandizing her work with the lame case management agency. Apparently after I kicked her out, she went and got drunk at a bar and then was assaulted. Ghosting her was difficult because she relentlessly pursued me for the purpose of providing the Sheriff's Department with a DNA sample. She wanted to press charges against her bar assailant, but his forensic evidence needed to be separated from mine from that same night. My conscience finally weighed on me enough to consent to the swabbing, and then I saw myself out of Vera's life for good. Footnote- If you ever go to a woman's house and she hasn't disabled "motion smoothing" (also known as the "soap opera effect") on her new television set then just leave. That's the default feature intended to make live sports look better, but causes movies to look worse. Get your shit together, Vera.

Back in the future, Vera suddenly appeared on one of my cases as one of those state auditors that doesn't really supply any contribution of value to the lives of children and their families. About as soon as I recognized her name, my phone rang and Vera was on the other line ready to gloat about her superior position. She said she found me working the same job I kicked her out of my apartment for glorifying was ironic. I told her I invented a boys group so my job was more fulfilling than when she did the same thing only worse, and that I was actually a high school teacher who was temporarily transplanted to mental and behavioral health while COVID-19 ran its course. Vera started bossing me around in regards to the client we shared, and I let the phone drop to my side wishing I could just kick her out of my apartment again. When she finished talking, I told her I was going to ask that this case be reassigned due to our past personal relationship. She called my site and asked to speak with the "supervisor of the day" to complain. That just made her look stupid, and Karen and Quintessa reassigned the case while laughing about an ex-girlfriend of mine acting hysterical and crazy. Although I got what I wanted, I realized I benefited from the patriarchy (even though Karen and Quintessa are women) and was probably in the wrong. Vera's OK. I just didn't want to work with her again, and talking to her reminded me that case management jobs are beneath me (and everyone who isn't Vera).

I was looking for a reason to quit when two events made me realize the time was right. The first event was when Karen fired Quintessa. Karen was a bumbling fool who stepped up to direct our site after our site had been running itself just fine for months. Lame case management agencies and their corporate layers are so damn top heavy there is always another bumbling fool piled on until the whole company collapses under its own weight. Karen toiled at dumb shit like scheduling unnecessary meetings, asking us without authenticity if we remembered our self care, setting up hot coco tables instead of advocating for staff raises, and forcing people back into the office before reversing herself because COVID-19 still spreads like wildfire. Watching Karen talk to poor minority women in the lobby was always hilarious, especially when one of them would give her a piece of their mind, "Best get out of my face, white bitch!" That never got old to me. Anyway, Karen fired Quintessa when Quintessa finally decided that she might want to scale back her work and spend more time with her own kids. Quintessa said she was open to part time employment, and Karen called security to escort her out of the office in tears. The second event was when a coworker showed me that our lame case management agency jacked up its starting pay for our position to try and make up for nobody wanting to take the job. The evidence was all over our company's postings on popular job seeking websites. Incensed, I went to Karen and asked when my pay was going to be increased to what the new people would be making. She chuckled, and told me, "That's not how that works."

Ya boy went back to his cubicle and thought for a moment, "No, that is how this works." I looked over my caseload and triple-checked that all my new clients waiting to leave the hospital after suicide attempts had completed referrals for outpatient services then I went on a farewell tour around the office. I told Horatio, Nika and Amy goodbye without them knowing I was about to fuck off forever. I walked back to my cubicle, and left my keys, FOB, badge, laptop and phone on my desk. I drove home then remotely logged into my email and sent a message to my entire site. In my screed, I said I was going to get drunk and never come back. I blind copied my work wife (different site) for cool points. And then I got drunk and never again worked at the lame case management agency. The outpouring of support from suddenly former coworkers was overwhelming. Somehow my personal number spread around, and I learned that everybody hated their jobs as much as I did. I knew I did the right thing because if people like me who can walk away from a bad deal don't walk away then nothing will ever get better. Karen now has to pay some new person the higher rate to replace me, and my replacement won't be half as effective. Or even a quarter as sexy. I quit on Friday, and the relief I felt not going back on Monday was orgasmic.

I BECOME A REAL TEACHER

Part 46

I still love unemployment

I used to be patriotic. Unfortunately, seeing the American flag these days conjures up images of hillbillies and rednecks spewing COVID-19 from their mouths onto the faces of our essential workers. And of course "essential workers" is subterfuge for modern slaves. The United States of America is a failed state. My lovely little brick apartments were just bought out by the evil company that wrecked my credit after I fled from it. My rent was raised over $100, and I'm expecting that to happen again next year (and I half expect to be flagged for eviction due to my history with this evil company). Fuck this shit so hard. The USA could be a paradise, but instead we have $18 an hour jobs and global warming. The world's cumulative advancements have reached a crescendo where we could easily be living in a post-poverty utopia where everybody's basic needs are guaranteed from birth, and the planet's existence is protected for our children and grandchildren! But, no. We have billionaires hoarding the wealth and imprisoning us in misery. We have hillbillies and rednecks wearing red hats because they can't critically think about how they are being used and abused. Why don't we have three days off every weekend? The science tells us we need one day to rest, one day to catch up on chores, and one day to pursue our hobbies. The 40 hour work week should immediately be scaled back to 32 hours, and $18 an hour should likewise be changed to $22.50 an hour. And that's just to start! The people who don't want to work should not have to work. We have the technology and resources to make that happen. If the government takes away our ability to freely live off the land then that same government needs to provide for our basic needs. Full stop.

I slipped back into unemployed life like I never left, and my days were glorious! Remember, while working at the Hummingbird Academy I was on a contract that included paychecks throughout summer vacation. Except I skipped taking a summer vacation and immediately went to work at the lame case management agency. So I basically had three months worth of double paychecks which now amounted to the ability to chill all over again. I had so much fun! So. Much. Fun. I was nervous to tell Sky I rage quit my job, but she understood my reasoning and didn't react negatively. In fact, she was down to make the most of my newly opened schedule. We went hiking, we attended shows, we ate at restaurants, we made love, and we once occupied a table at a coffee shop for hours with a space colonizing boardgame she owns that uses, like, a million tiny pieces. We sat at a food truck by her house and befriended its Thai entrepreneur. This guy was pursuing food as his passion while working a day job somewhere else (see, people would still work even if they weren't forced into wage slavery, but they would just do what makes them happy which actually benefits all of us). He told us when he came to America he wanted his children to have names that blended in with their classmates so he named his first son Donald. Our new friend said this choice became unfortunate when Donald Rumsfeld splashed into our lives, and became unfortunate again when... do I really have to tell you? You already know who splashed into our lives next. Not working makes me so happy. I cannot wait until these glimpses of freedom the pandemic provided become the status quo. Or, you know, we all die in the climate wars.

While living the dream, I left my various online resumes set to "looking for work" and entertained a never ending stream of solicitations for new, equally shitty, $18 an hour jobs. Sometimes I would answer just to screw with hiring managers and HR departments. Another time I went to the interview because the building was only a block away from my apartments and I thought the ability to walk to work would make wage slaving more palatable. When the two goons at this lame (lamer) case management agency sitting in a strip mall started telling me that the intense paperwork doesn't feel intense because of all the good accomplished I just laughed and headed for the door. I also had to pee, and when I asked for the restrooms they handed me a key because their toilets were in an annex. So returning the bathroom key after prematurely ending the interview was awkward. On second thought, the cringe was hilarious! Nothing mattered anymore because I finally figured out that working is a complete joke. I used to stress about the appearance of my resume because I tend to rage quit a lot, but then I realized there is no penalty for lying. So I deleted the jobs that were less than a year in length and added that time to the jobs where I stayed longer. My experience is real (case management, supervising, foster care, and substance abuse counseling), but my job history is neatly repackaged into three main jobs. Nobody checks. I even passed a third party background screening to get hired at a global non-profit which I ultimately decided not to work at when my colleague already working there told me that management was as toxic and abusive as anywhere else. Did the professional screeners not do their jobs? They probably get paid $18 an hour and truly don't give a fuck. How can anyone be excited to work for a pittance? The system is broken.

I planned on staying unemployed for six months, but a surprisingly worthwhile opportunity appeared only three weeks into my newly rediscovered joy.

Part 47

I get my own Freshman classroom

I received flattering outreach from a "better" charter school. Fox High School was still a charter school, but a close facsimile to a real school in that there were buses, classes, lunch, sports, a bell schedule, actual desks, white boards with dry erase markers, physical books, a sprawling campus with benches, amenities, assembly areas, clubs and cheerleaders. Fox sat on the opposite side of the freeway from the Hummingbird Academy, and also offered low income Hispanic students an accelerated high school diploma. The difference was that Hummingbird distilled education down to computer clicks then wondered why students and staff developed psychological problems. Fox took a class like English, which is what I teach, and divided the entire year into four blocks. The Freshman, Sophomore, Junior and Senior English curriculum stretches through three blocks each, keeping that fourth block free to fix anything that goes wrong. A student can't fail an entire English class, he or she can only fail a block of English and then make up whatever is missing in the last block (usually with a para-pro or instructional aide). Students also only attend three classes a day, and have all that time in the afternoon for mandatory tutoring if their grades drop. Students feel like they are attending a regular high school, but with more safety nets and speed. I'm sure there's an evil corporate schemer up top shaking hands with an evil government schemer so none of these impoverished students slip through the cracks without a high school diploma and miss out on the ability to work for slave wages, but as far as providing an alternative education the Fox approach is superior.

Here is an example of how a student might finish four years of English in three years with blocks:

School Year 21-22	Freshman English	Freshman English	Freshman English	Sophomore English
School Year 22-23	Sophomore English	Sophomore English	Junior English	Junior English
School Year 23-24	Junior English	Senior English	Senior English	Senior English
School Year 24-25				

The teachers don't know which class they will teach in their fourth block until the year gets that far, because some of the responsibility to pass classes quickly rests with the students themselves. The admin tracks student success and responds to needs early so teachers get to stay in their lanes and mostly feel like real teachers with logically unfolding classes.

I had some history with Fox High School because I visited once or twice while working at Esperanza Siempre. I would come visit individual students for their drug counseling, and the principal was always beyond accommodating. She would find us an office, sometimes even her office, and encourage us to take as much time as we needed. When she called me so soon after I rage quit the lame case management agency, I was more inclined to talk now than stick with my previous plan of spending upwards of six months unemployed. I knew this opportunity was probably a worthwhile chance to resurrect my dream of earning my state teaching certificate in a charter school without falling in with another dump like Hummingbird. Principal Filiberta scheduled a same day video interview, and by the end of the conversation she said she would try and get me approved to teach Freshman English. If corporate said no, she asked if I would be interested in discussing either the social worker or dropout prevention specialist positions. Sure, why not?

Principal Filiberta called back sooner than expected and wanted to meet again, but I had to push her off a day because I already planned to go hiking with Sky. We video conferenced the following morning, and Principal Filiberta confirmed that corporate counted up the English credits in my journalism degree and cleared me to teach Freshman English. She invited me to a posh breakfast with herself and the vice-principal, and then I got to see my classroom. My real classroom. Not a traumatizing digital sweatshop. I looked around the 35 desks, the poster of William Shakespeare, the cabinet full of laptops if we needed them, my desk, my lectern, and my overall sphere of influence. Wow! This is the classroom I had in mind when I attended the Department of Education Career Fair all that time ago. I felt a swell of pride.

I think, as of writing, I'm three months into my Freshman English stint at Fox High School and I don't regret giving up my dream to stay unemployed longer. I did learn something shitty yesterday while talking with the Junior English teacher. She started teaching here four years ago, and is currently making $41,000 a year. I started three months ago and am making $48,000 a year. Ugh. Just fucking pay people! My colleague told me that Fox High School felt the effects of the Great Resignation and responded by jacking up pay for new hires, but not loyal teachers already there (sound familiar?). I shared this phenomenon was exactly the reason why I left the lame case management agency, and encouraged her to consider job hopping to a better salary. Even though I like Fox High School, my job seeking profiles are still attracting offers and the amounts keep getting bigger. Most recently I was approached for a full time substitute position in Tucson's biggest school district at a whopping $38 an hour. Sounds like the money was available all along, and America just needs to fucking pay its people! I don't care if we call spreading the wealth socialism or something else, but nobody should be forced to work full time just to struggle. I like that maxim saying if we discovered a monkey hoarding all the bananas while all the other moneys starved to death then we would study the killer monkey to find out what went wrong in its brain. Unfortunately, in the course of teaching Freshman English I do occasionally catch myself sounding like a hypocritical capitalist. I see over 100 students a day, and sometimes say, "Stop talking to each other and get back to work, if you can't manage 90 minutes of self control now you'll never survive the demands of a good job." Gross. Hopefully, this generation is the one to bring back guillotines and drag billionaires from their yachts.

Part 48

I think I'm OK

After Principal Filiberta and her vice-principal took me to that fancy breakfast, the type of place where my mom dines, they warned that I may not be able to start soon due to outstanding training obligations. Obviously that got reversed and I've been teaching without the corporate training courses ever since. Sometimes I just stop and laugh over getting hired to teach children twice (or three times with substitute teaching), and nobody ever checked on me at all at Hummingbird or for months at Fox. When the admin at Fox did finally observe me teaching, I was awarded four out of seven stars (nailed it). Despite hating the system for which I am forced to participate, I do enjoy my newest job. Or at least I am content to know I could be suffering a lot more. I teach three 90 minute classes back-to-back-to-back and then have the rest of my day to sit in my classroom and grade papers and make plans. My classroom quickly became the cool classroom to hang out during the open tutoring time and, while that can be annoying, I'm flattered to see my room fill up with the happy faces. Or at least the top half of the happy faces because masks are mandatory. The hardest adjustment was probably waking up early and training my bladder. I make sure I've swallowed my last drop of coffee by 5:30 a.m. so I can pee for the last time at 7:30 a.m. and then I do not drink again until I've said goodbye to third period.

What am I teaching my Freshmen? Well, when I'm in front of the room I think I'm spending, on average, a third of the time on actual Language Arts curriculum, a third of the time on counseling topics based on whatever issues my kids bring in from home, and a third of the time on general life skills since I am full of all this stellar wisdom. Thanks to leaving the Hummingbird Academy with all of Mr. Pecker's slideshows, I have a never ending wellspring of educational material. When the corporate curriculum map tells me I need to be teaching "rhetoric" next week, I check my folder and (score!) there's a Mr. Pecker slideshow for that. Sometimes the students can be annoying, I mean, there are almost 40 of them squeezed in there at a time, but they always come back and cover whatever they did to piss me off with genuine flattery. I hear that I am somebody's favorite teacher at least once a day. I also get asked why I'm a white person a lot. Sorry, kids, that can't be helped.

I don't know what else to say. These chapters are getting shorter and harder to write as my mental and emotional pain subsides. I guess that was the point when I started suicide journaling a few months ago. This isn't a real book, anyway. If the last chapter is only a sentence long then the last chapter is only a sentence long. I like teaching Freshman English. I enjoy going on two dates a week with Sky (one date is an activity, and the other date is a sex date). I smile over my friendship with my ex-work wife. I'm fulfilled by my friendship with Marketplace Madison. Both of those ladies have read the rough draft of my book. Sky is loosely aware that I am writing something, but she doesn't know the content is filth. I'm not looking forward to that coming out. I do still think about she-who-will-no-longer-be-mentioned-by-name, but my thoughts no longer get stuck on her when I'm working or trying to do other things. I can postpone my memories and then engage with them late at night. I wonder if the man she replaced me with is a cuck who doesn't care about genital herpes because accepting the risk is the only way he will access a relationship with somebody amazing. Then I feel guilty for thinking that and hope for her that this guy is wonderful without worry. Maybe he already had HSV-2 and they never think about precautions. I get sad that there was a biological barrier in me that made the thought of knowingly exposing myself to genital herpes revolting, but that's probably because I overthink everything. After all my research, I really don't think having the infection would be that bad. I just want to avoid blisters on my penis as long as possible. If I had to get stabbed in the heart over this to meet my ex-work wife, Marketplace Madison and Sky then I'd knowingly go through everything again.

Part 49

I finally catch COVID-19

This penultimate chapter was unplanned, but fitting. I'm sitting here winding down my book whilst simultaneously recovering from COVID-19. After two years spent avoiding COVID, the chase is over. COVID got me. I waited in a short line of cars at the community college yesterday, and if the emailed results are still positive on the PCR test then my time away from work is paid out from some kind of bucket of emergency PTO. If the PCR says I'm negative then I don't qualify for emergency PTO, but was still forced to stay home because of my original positive rapid test. The time to myself has been amazing (you know I love these microcosms of unemployment), and I am truly unbothered by whether the week is paid or unpaid other than the uncertainty agitates my main complaint that we as a people are being exploited by the ruling class of billionaires. What would a government of the people, by the people, and for the people actually look like? Maybe one day we should find out. I can't imagine anybody I know voting for features like unpaid lunches. We would probably vote to clock in before starting the commute and not clock out until returning home. Actually, thinking in terms of clocking in and out is probably all wrong. This is not the way to live.

My COVID experience isn't so harrowing thanks to the doctors, scientists, researchers and, yes, maybe a few decent politicians who worked hard to get us here. I've had the vaccine three times by now, and only got curious about my symptoms when my energy never picked up after my third period class last Friday. I teach over one hundred students a day, and a large chunk of them have been riding the COVID merry-go-round. I knew I was going to get it. I came home to start the weekend, and couldn't shake the feeling of fatigue. Pizza didn't help. Beer didn't help. Masturbation didn't help. Mostly out of ideas, I went to bed early and then woke up still tired. I drank my coffee, ate my donuts, and tried masturbating one more time. Nothing helped. I still felt run down like I never recuperated from my week at work. I took a long nap, and woke up tired. I never lost my appetite so I visited a fast food drive through again. Sunday was similar to Saturday in that I could eat whatever I wanted, but felt unrested and sluggish. I decided to take one of the two free COVID tests I had lying around, and my eyes widened when that line appeared across the part of the stick labeled positive. Not that I was too shocked, all things considered, but my positive result was the final confirmation that I couldn't outrun the inevitable forever. I texted a photo to my principal, and apologized for spoiling her weekend. She wished me well, told me I wouldn't be allowed to come to school for a few days, and then tacked on the part about needing a PCR test if I wanted to be paid.

Sunday night, I figured I better deviate from junk food long enough to nourish myself out of COVID. My normal diet works against my immune system so I went and bought a bag of eight pears. A lot of pear was lost when I cut the eight of them into spears, but I still consumed a huge pile of fruit and went to bed. Monday I had diarrhea most of the day. Yeah, probably because of the bag of pears. Tuesday I experienced burning in my throat and some discomfort swallowing, and for a split second remembered reports that COVID can come in light and stay light for a deceptive amount of time before turning heavy. By Wednesday, I mostly felt refreshed and back to normal. No longer tired, I put all my pocket monster equipment in my backpack and went out on a community expedition. I wore my mask around other people just in case they weren't vaccinated. Tomorrow, I'll find out what my students did to the substitute teacher.

In the end, my time off was paid.

Part 50

One Year Later…

Close enough! We're still about three months away from one year since I left the Hummingbird Academy, but that's what I wanted to call this chapter. Mr. Spudspank is still the glue that holds us all together, and those of us who trauma bonded under the abuse from Principal Hillbilly still occasionally hang out because of him. The Hummingbird Academy finally broke Mr. Spudspank and, he likes to say, turned him into me and Mr. Dutch. I like to say he just became the best version of himself. Mr. Spudspank led the rebellion the school year after I left, and everybody except Ms. Catgastro quit. Seriously, what self respecting adult is going to let a fat hillbilly tell them they can't sit down for $18 an hour? They all easily found better jobs. Principal Hillbilly cried in her office after everyone walked out, and then doubled down on the academic fraud by rehiring Ms. Moon. My students at Fox High School hear rumors that another charter school exists across the freeway where students are considered customers, don't wear masks, and can graduate just by clicking on a computer screen. I warn them that they won't like the digital sweatshop, and hope they listen.

The end.

Made in the USA
Middletown, DE
07 July 2022

68149755R00116